Dr Eliot Attridge • Nathan Goodman • Susan Loxley •

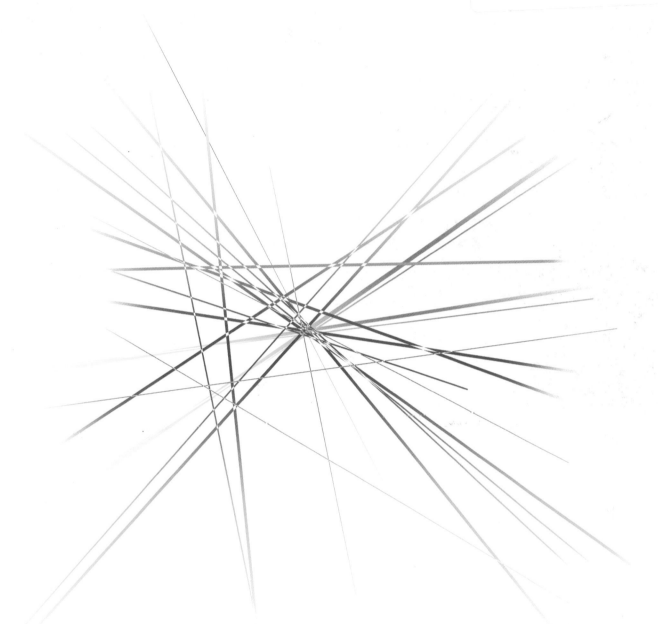

ESSENTIALS

OCR Twenty First Century
GCSE Additional Science
Revision Guide

Contents

Contents

Acknowledgements

Acknowledgements

The authors and publisher would like to thank everyone who has contributed to this book:

p.35   ©iStockphoto.com / Matthew Cole
p.75   ©iStockphoto.com / Royce DeGrie
p.77   ©iStockphoto.com / Edward Murphy
        ©iStockphoto.com / Kim Bryant
p.85   ©iStockphoto.com / Dawn Hudson
p.110 ©iStockphoto.com / Luis Carlos Torres
p.111 ©iStockphoto.com
p.115 ©iStockphoto.com
        ©iStockphoto.com / Russell Tate

ISBN 978-1-905896-42-4

Published by Lonsdale, a division of Huveaux Plc.

Authors: Dr Eliot Attridge
Nathan Goodman
Susan Loxley
Dr Dorothy Warren

Project Editor: Michelle l'Anson

Cover Design: Angela English

Concept Design: Sarah Duxbury and Helen Jacobs

Designer: Paul Oates

Artwork: Lonsdale and HL Studios

Author Information

Dr Eliot Attridge (Biology) is a full member of the Institute of Biology, a chartered biologist (CBiol), and an experienced Head of Science. He works closely with the exam board as an Assistant Examiner for OCR Twenty First Century Science and was involved in writing the scheme of work for the new GCSE. His school, having been involved in the pilot, has now implemented the new GCSE.

Nathan Goodman (Physics) has an in-depth understanding of the new science specifications, thanks to his roles as Secondary Science Strategy Consultant for North East Lincolnshire LEA and Regional Coordinator at the Institute of Physics for the Physics Teacher Network. As an Assistant Headteacher, Nathan is involved in improving the teaching and learning of science at his school.

Susan Loxley (Chemistry) has an excellent understanding of the applications of science in industry, having been involved in the development of materials for aerospace for eight years. She now teaches chemistry to Key Stage 3 and Key Stage 4 pupils and is an examiner for GCSE science.

Dr Dorothy Warren (Chemistry) is a member of the Royal Society of Chemistry, a former science teacher, and a Secondary Science Consultant with the Quality and Improvement Service for North Yorkshire County Council. Having been involved in the pilot scheme for OCR Twenty First Century Science, she has an excellent understanding of the new specifications, which she has helped to implement in local schools.

This revision guide has been written and developed to help you get the most out of your revision.

This guide covers both Foundation and Higher Tier content.

(HT) Content that will only be tested on the Higher Tier papers appears in a pale yellow tinted box labelled with the (HT) symbol.

- The **coloured page headers** clearly identify the separate units, so that you can revise for each exam separately: Biology is red, Chemistry is purple, and Physics is blue.
- There are **practice questions** at the end of each unit so you can test yourself on what you've just learned. (The answers are given on pages 125–127 so you can mark your own answers.)

- You'll find **key words** in a yellow box on each two-page spread. They are also highlighted in colour within the text; Higher Tier key words are highlighted in orange. Make sure you know and understand all these words before moving on!
- There's a **glossary** at the back of the book. It contains all the key words from throughout the book so you can check any definitions you're not sure about.
- The **tick boxes** on the contents page let you track your revision progress: simply put a tick in the box next to each topic when you're confident that you know it.
- Don't just read the guide, **learn actively**! Constantly test yourself without looking at the text.

Good luck with your exams!

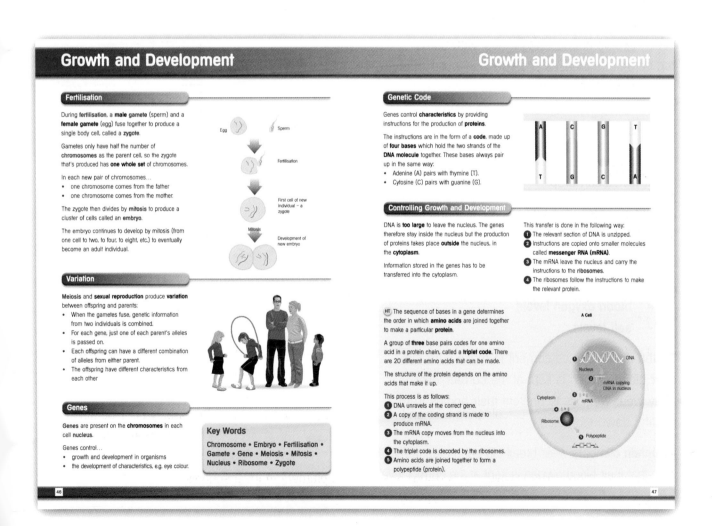

Homeostasis

Homeostasis

Homeostasis is the maintenance of a constant internal environment. It's achieved by...
- balancing bodily inputs and outputs
- removing waste products.

Your body has **automatic control systems** which maintain steady levels of...
- **temperature**
- **water** (**hydration**).

These factors enable your cells to function properly.

The failure of homeostasis results in death.

Factors Affecting Homeostasis

Homeostasis can be affected by...
- exercise
- the temperature of your surroundings.

When you do strenuous exercise, your body temperature increases and you lose water through sweat. Your body needs to get rid of the excess heat and replace the lost water so that your systems will continue to work correctly.

In **hot climates** your body temperature can rise and water levels can drop.

In **cold climates** your body loses heat and this can lead to **hypothermia**.

(HT) Homeostasis can also be affected by changes in...
- **blood oxygen levels**
- **salt levels.**

Scuba divers use equipment to make sure that their blood oxygen is kept at the correct level. They wear wetsuits to prevent their bodies from cooling down too much.

Mountain climbers wear breathing apparatus to make sure that their blood oxygen is kept at the correct level.

Key Words

Effector • Homeostasis • Hypothermia • Incubator • Receptor

Artificial Homeostasis

Artificial homeostasis is needed when the body's control systems don't work correctly.

For example, an **incubator** helps a premature baby to survive by controlling its temperature and oxygen levels.

Artificial systems and body systems both have…
- **receptors** (sensors) to detect stimuli
- **processing centres** to receive information and coordinate responses
- **effectors** which automatically produce the response.

HT Negative Feedback

Negative feedback works to maintain a **steady state**. When the conditions rise above / fall beneath a set level, the response is to reverse the direction of change.

When the temperature inside an incubator **exceeds** a set level, the following happens:
1. Temperature rise is detected by a sensor (**receptor**).
2. The **processing centre** in the computer responds by sending a signal to the heater.
3. The heater (**effector**) turns off.

The temperature inside the incubator may then **drop below** a set level and the following happens:
1. Fall in temperature is detected by a sensor (**receptor**).
2. The **processing centre** in the computer responds by sending a signal to the heater.
3. The heater (**effector**) turns on.

Conditions in the body change from set point

Change detected

Corrective response activated

Conditions return to set point

Corrective response switched off

Antagonistic Effectors

In many systems there are effectors that act **antagonistically** (i.e. as opposites) to one another.

For example, one effector is responsible for increasing temperature whilst another is responsible for decreasing the temperature.

This method of control is far more sensitive and accurate.

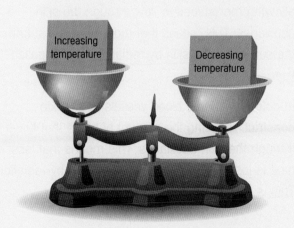

Increasing temperature

Decreasing temperature

Homeostasis

Body Temperature

Energy loss and **energy gain** from your body need to be balanced so that your body temperature remains **constant**.

The temperature of your body's extremities tends to be cooler than your core body temperature. Energy is transferred from the **blood** to the **tissues** when it reaches the cooler parts.

Controlling body temperature requires...

- **temperature receptors in the skin** to detect the external temperature
- **temperature receptors in the brain** to measure the temperature of the blood
- **the brain** which acts as a processing centre, to receive information from the temperature receptors, responding by triggering the **effectors**
- effectors (sweat glands and muscles) to carry out the automatic response.

If your body temperature is **too high**, heat needs to be transferred to the environment. This is done by **sweating**, since **evaporation** from the skin requires heat energy from the body.

If your body temperature is **too low**, your body will start to **shiver**. Shivering is the rapid **contraction** and release of muscles. These contractions require energy from increased **respiration**, and heat is released as a by-product, warming surrounding tissue.

(HT) Vasodilation and Vasoconstriction

Blood temperature is monitored by a centre in your brain called the hypothalamus.

In **hot conditions**, blood vessels in the skin **dilate**, allowing more blood to flow through the skin capillaries. This means that more heat is lost from the surface of the skin by radiation. This is called vasodilation.

In **cold conditions**, blood vessels in the skin **constrict**, reducing the amount of blood that flows through the skin capillaries. This means that less heat is lost from the surface of the skin by radiation. This is called vasoconstriction.

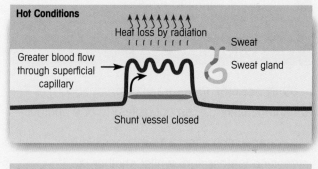

Hot Conditions

Heat loss by radiation

Sweat

Greater blood flow through superficial capillary

Sweat gland

Shunt vessel closed

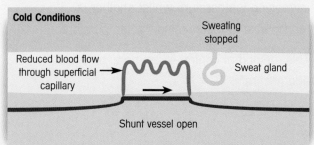

Cold Conditions

Sweating stopped

Reduced blood flow through superficial capillary

Sweat gland

Shunt vessel open

Heat Stroke

Heat stroke is an **uncontrolled** increase in your body temperature.

Increased sweating due to very hot temperatures can lead to **dehydration**. Dehydration stops sweating from occurring which leads to the core body temperature increasing even further.

If your body isn't cooled down, the normal systems for controlling body temperature break down and this results in death.

Causes of heat stroke include…
- exercising in very warm conditions
- very high humidity
- dehydration.

Symptoms of heat stroke are…
- confusion
- red/dry skin
- low blood pressure
- convulsions
- fainting
- rapid heartbeat.

Initially, you can treat heat stroke by…
- removing clothes and bathing in cool water
- cooling body using wet towels
- using a fan
- putting ice packs on the neck, head and groin
- elevating (raising) the legs.

Hypothermia

Hypothermia occurs when your body is exposed to **low temperatures** for a long period of time. Your body can't replace heat as fast as it's being lost and, if untreated, this can lead to death.

The common cause of hypothermia is when your **core body temperature** falls below **35°C**.

Symptoms of hypothermia are…
- grey skin colour
- amnesia (memory loss)
- shivering
- slurred speech
- confusion
- loss of coordination
- cold skin.

Initially, you can treat hypothermia by…
- raising the core body temperature
- insulating the body (particularly the armpits, head and groin)
- drinking warm drinks, but not alcohol.

N.B. You shouldn't rub or massage the skin – this brings blood to the surface, causing even more heat to be lost.

Key Words

Effector • Hypothalamus • **Hypothermia** • **Receptor** • Vasoconstriction • Vasodilation

Homeostasis

Water Balance

Water is **input** (gained) from…
- food and drinks
- respiration.

Water is **output** (lost) through…
- sweating
- breathing
- excretion of faeces and urine.

Your body has to **balance** these different inputs and outputs to ensure that there's enough water inside cells for cell activity to take place.

The Kidneys

Your kidneys filter your blood to remove **urea** (waste) and to balance levels of other chemicals (including water) transported in the blood plasma. They achieve this by…
- filtering small molecules from your blood to form urine (water, salt and urea)
- reabsorbing all the sugar
- reabsorbing as much salt as your body needs
- reabsorbing as much water as your body needs
- excreting remaining urine, stored in your **bladder**.

Right kidney

Left kidney

Bladder

Regulating Water Levels

Your kidneys balance the water level in your body:
- When the water level is **too high**, your kidneys reabsorb less water and a **large amount of dilute urine** is produced.
- When the water level is **too low**, your kidneys reabsorb more water and a **small amount of concentrated urine** is produced.

The amount of water that needs to reabsorbed into the blood plasma depends on…
- the external temperature
- the amount of exercise taken
- the fluid intake.

When **salt levels** increase, your body removes any excess salt by producing dilute urine. This means you need to intake more fluids to maintain a balanced water level.

Alcohol causes a large amount of dilute urine to be produced. This can lead to **dehydration**.

Ecstasy causes a small amount of concentrated urine to be produced.

Key Words

Anti-diuretic hormone • Hypothalamus • Pituitary gland • **Urea**

(HT) Anti-Diuretic Hormone

The concentration of urine is controlled by a hormone called anti-diuretic hormone (**ADH**), which is released into your blood via the pituitary gland.

Controlling water balance is an example of **negative feedback**.

When your blood water level becomes **too high** (i.e. there's too much water) the following happens:

1. Receptors in your hypothalamus detect a decrease in salt concentration. No stimulus is sent to the pituitary gland.
2. Less ADH is secreted into the blood.
3. Your kidneys become **less permeable** so less water is reabsorbed.
4. Your bladder fills with a **large quantity of dilute urine**.

If your blood water level becomes **too low** (i.e. not enough water) the opposite happens:

1. Receptors in your **hypothalamus** detect an increase in salt concentration. A stimulus is sent to the pituitary gland. **Thirst** is stimulated to encourage drinking.
2. More ADH is secreted into the blood.
3. Your kidneys become **more permeable** so more water is reabsorbed.
4. Your bladder fills with a **small quantity of concentrated urine**.

Diagram

Normal blood water level

Blood

| High blood water level | | Low blood water level |

Hypothalamus

| Receptors detect change | | Receptors detect change |

Pituitary gland

| Less ADH secreted | | More ADH secreted |

Kidneys

| Kidneys reabsorb less water | | Kidneys reabsorb more water |

Bladder

| Large quantity of dilute urine produced | | Small quantity of concentrated urine produced |

Normal blood water level

ADH and Drugs

Drugs such as alcohol and Ecstasy affect the production of ADH in different ways:

- **Alcohol** causes ADH to be **suppressed**, so more water leaves the body in the urine.
- **Ecstasy** causes **too much** ADH to be produced, so too much water remains in the blood. Osmosis then causes the water to leave the blood causing brain cells to swell and burst.

Homeostasis

Diffusion

Diffusion is the overall movement of **substances** from regions of **high** concentration, to regions of **low** concentration.

Substances that move in and out of cells by diffusion include…
- oxygen (O_2)
- carbon dioxide (CO_2)
- dissolved food.

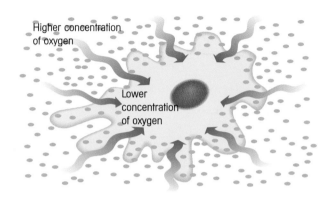

Higher concentration of oxygen

Lower concentration of oxygen

(HT) Active Transport

Some chemicals can also be moved by active transport. This is the movement of a substance against a concentration gradient (i.e. from a region of low concentration to high concentration). It requires **energy** to do this.

For example, if the concentration of glucose inside a cell is higher than the concentration outside the cell, the glucose would diffuse out of the cell along the concentration gradient. So, cells use active transport to bring all of the glucose back inside the cell.

Osmosis

Osmosis is a type of diffusion. It's the overall movement of **water** from a **dilute solution** to a more **concentrated solution** through a partially permeable membrane.

The membrane allows the passage of water molecules but not solute molecules, which are too large.

Osmosis gradually **dilutes** the concentrated solution.

(HT) Animal cells, unlike plant cells, don't have a cell wall, which supports the cell membrane, so osmosis can have serious effects:
- If **too much water** enters, the cell could rupture.
- If a **cell loses a lot of water** it won't be able to carry out chemical reactions.

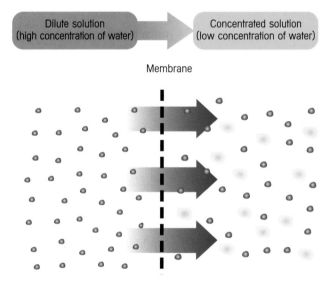

Dilute solution (high concentration of water)

Concentrated solution (low concentration of water)

Membrane

Key Words

Active site • Active transport • **Denatured enzyme** • **Diffusion** • **Enzyme** • **Osmosis**

Enzymes

Enzymes are protein molecules that speed up the rate of chemical reactions in cells (i.e. catalysts in living things).

Enzymes need a specific temperature to work at their **optimum**. Different enzymes have different optimum working temperatures. The graph shows the effect of **temperature** on enzyme activity:

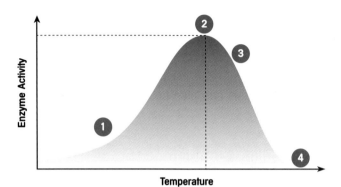

1. At low temperatures, small increases in temperature cause an increase in the frequency and energy of collisions between reactants and enzymes, so the rate of reaction increases.
2. The **optimum enzyme activity** is reached.
3. After the optimum enzyme activity is reached, the enzymes start to get damaged.
4. The enzyme becomes **denatured** (its structure is permanently destroyed and it stops working).

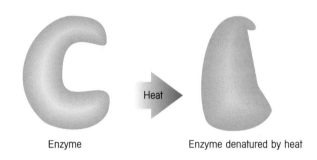

Enzyme   Enzyme denatured by heat

The Lock and Key Model

Only a molecule with the correct shape can fit into an enzyme. This is a bit like a **key** (the molecule) fitting into a **lock** (the enzyme). Once the enzyme and molecule are linked, the following happens:

1. The reaction takes place.
2. The products are released.
3. The process is able to start again.

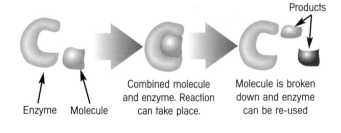

Products

Enzyme   Molecule | Combined molecule and enzyme. Reaction can take place. | Molecule is broken down and enzyme can be re-used

HT The Active Site

The active site is the place where the molecule fits into the enzyme. Each enzyme has a different **shape**, so it's highly specific.

The shape of the active site can be changed irreversibly by…

- **heating** the enzyme above a certain temperature
- altering the **pH level**.

This means the molecule can no longer fit and the reaction can't take place.

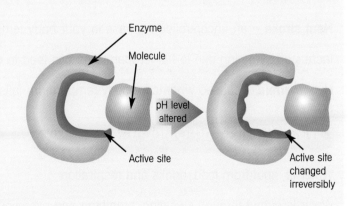

Enzyme

Molecule

pH level altered

Active site

Active site changed irreversibly

Module B4 Summary

Homeostasis

Homeostasis = maintenance of a constant internal environment.

Homeostasis can be affected by **exercise** and **temperature**.

(HT) Homeostasis can also be affected by **blood oxygen levels** and **salt levels**.

Controlling Conditions

Artificial homeostasis – needed when the body's control systems don't work correctly.

Incubators – help premature babies to survive by controlling **temperature** and **oxygen levels**.

Artificial systems and body systems have…
*   receptors
*   processing centres
*   effectors.

(HT) **Negative feedback** – maintenance of a steady state by reversing the change in conditions.

Antagonistic effectors – act as opposites to one another.

Body Temperature

Hot climates ➡ body temperature too high ➡ **sweating**.

Cold climates ➡ body temperature too low ➡ **shivering**.

(HT) **Hypothalamus** – part of the brain responsible for maintaining homeostasis.

Vasodilation = blood vessels in skin dilate in **hot conditions**.

Vasoconstriction = blood vessels in skin constrict in **cold conditions**.

Heat stroke = an uncontrolled increase in your body temperature.

Increased sweating due to hot temperatures can lead to **dehydration**.

Hypothermia – caused when core body temperature falls below 35°C.

Water Inputs and Outputs

Water is input from food, drinks and respiration.

Water is output through sweating, breathing and excretion of faeces and urine.

Module B4 Summary

Water Balance

Kidneys – filter your blood to remove urea and to balance levels of water and other chemicals.

Water level high ➡ kidneys reabsorb less water ➡ large amount of dilute urine.

Water level low ➡ kidneys reabsorb more water ➡ small amount of concentrated urine.

Amount of water that needs to be reabsorbed into blood plasma depends on…
- external temperature
- exercise
- fluid intake
- salt intake.

Alcohol causes large amount of dilute urine to be produced.

Ecstasy causes small amount of concentrated urine to be produced.

HT **Anti-diuretic hormone** – controls concentration of urine. Released into your blood via the **pituitary gland**.

Alcohol ➡ ADH suppressed ➡ more water leaves the body in the urine.

Ecstasy ➡ too much ADH produced ➡ too much water remains in the blood.

Cells

Diffusion = movement of **substances** from high to low concentration.

Substances that move in and out of cells by diffusion include…
- oxygen
- carbon dioxide
- dissolved food.

Osmosis = movement of **water** from high to low concentration.

Active transport = movement of substances against a **concentration gradient** – requires **energy**.

Enzymes

Enzymes = protein molecules that speed up the rate of chemical reactions in cells (catalysts in living things).

Denatured enzyme = structure of the enzyme is permanently destroyed and stops working.

HT **Active site** = place where the molecule fits into the enzyme.

The shape of the active site is affected by…
- **heat**
- **pH level**.

Module B4 Practice Questions

1 Choose the correct words from the options given to complete the following sentence:

variable   **management**   **constant**   **conditions**   **environment**   **maintenance**

Homeostasis is the .... of a .... internal ....

2 What happens to the body if homeostasis fails?

....

3 If a person is doing strenuous exercise what two changes happen to the body? Tick the correct two options.

A Temperature of body decreases ⬭   **B** Temperature of body increases ⬭

C Water lost via sweat ⬭   **D** Water lost in urine ⬭

4 When in a cold climate there is a danger that homeostasis will start to fail. What condition does this cause? Tick the correct option.

A Hypothermia ⬭   **B** Warmth excess ⬭

C Flu ⬭   **D** Hyperthermia ⬭

HT **5** **a)** As well as exercise and temperature, homeostasis can be affected by two other factors. What are these factors?

i) ....   **ii)** ....

b) List two human activities which can affect these two factors.

i) ....   **ii)** ....

6 **a)** Match the words **A**, **B**, **C** and **D** with the spaces numbered **1−4** in the sentence below.

A effectors ....   **B** artificial ....

C receptors ....   **D** processing centres ....

Body systems and ......**1**...... systems have ......**2**...... to detect stimuli, ...**3**...... to receive

information and coordinate responses and ......**4**...... which produce the response automatically.

HT **b)** What is meant by the term negative feedback?

....

7 Name three substances which are moved in and out of cells by diffusion.

a) ....   **b)** ....   **c)** ....

8 This question is about enzymes.

a) On the axes draw the line of enzyme activity you would expect with a typical enzyme.

b) On the graph that you have drawn, add the letter A to show the optimum enzyme activity.

c) What is meant by the term denatured?

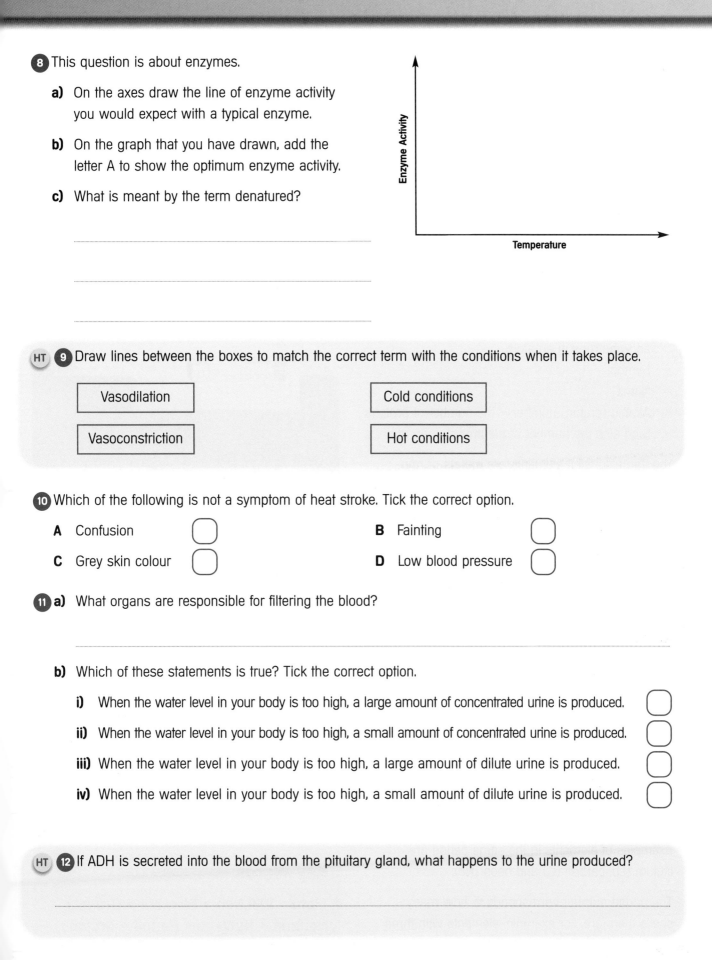

Enzyme Activity

Temperature

HT **9** Draw lines between the boxes to match the correct term with the conditions when it takes place.

| Vasodilation |

| Cold conditions |

| Vasoconstriction |

| Hot conditions |

10 Which of the following is not a symptom of heat stroke. Tick the correct option.

A Confusion ◯

B Fainting ◯

C Grey skin colour ◯

D Low blood pressure ◯

11 a) What organs are responsible for filtering the blood?

b) Which of these statements is true? Tick the correct option.

i) When the water level in your body is too high, a large amount of concentrated urine is produced. ◯

ii) When the water level in your body is too high, a small amount of concentrated urine is produced. ◯

iii) When the water level in your body is too high, a large amount of dilute urine is produced. ◯

iv) When the water level in your body is too high, a small amount of dilute urine is produced. ◯

HT **12** If ADH is secreted into the blood from the pituitary gland, what happens to the urine produced?

Chemical Patterns

The Periodic Table

An **element** is made of only one kind of **atom**. All the atoms of an element have the same number of **protons**.

Different **elements** have different **proton numbers** and they are arranged in order of ascending proton number in the **modern periodic table**.

This gives repeating **patterns** in the **properties** of elements.

You can use the periodic table as a reference table to obtain the following information about the elements:
- Relative atomic mass – total number of protons and **neutrons** in an atom.
- Symbol
- Name
- Atomic (proton) number – the number of protons (and also the number of **electrons**) in an atom.

You can also tell if elements are **metals** or **non-metals** by looking at their position in the table.

N.B. You will be given a copy of the periodic table in the exam.

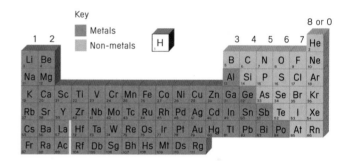

Groups

A **vertical column** of elements is called a **group**. Elements that are in the same group have **similar properties**.

Group 1 elements include…
- lithium (Li)
- sodium (Na)
- potassium (K).

The group number corresponds to the number of electrons in the outer shell of an atom. For example…
- **Group 1** elements have **1 electron** in the outer shell
- **Group 7** elements have **7 electrons** in their outer shell.

Periods

A **horizontal row** of elements is called a **period**. Examples of elements in the same period are lithium (Li), carbon (C) and neon (Ne).

The period number corresponds to how many shells there are. For example, elements with three shells are found in the third period.

Key Words

Atom • Electron • Element • Group • Neutron • Nucleus • Period • Proton

Atoms

An **atom** has a **small central nucleus**, made up of **protons** and **neutrons**.

The nucleus is surrounded by **electrons** which are arranged in **shells** (**energy levels**).

An atom has the same number of protons as electrons, so the atom as a whole is **neutral** (i.e. it has no electrical charge).

A proton has the same **mass** as a neutron. The mass of an electron is **negligible** (nearly 0).

All atoms of the same element have the same number of protons.

Atomic Particle	Relative Mass	Relative Charge
Proton	1	+1
Neutron	1	0
Electron	0 (nearly)	−1

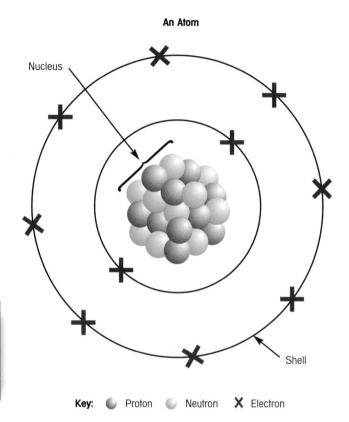

An Atom

Nucleus

Shell

Key: Proton   Neutron X Electron

Spectroscopy

Some elements emit distinctive coloured flames when they're heated, for example....
- lithium – red
- sodium – yellow
- potassium – lilac.

The light emitted from the flame of an element produces a characteristic **line spectrum**.

Each line in the spectrum represents an energy change as electrons fall from high energy levels to lower energy levels.

Scientists realised some time ago that each element has its own unique spectrum.

The study of **spectra** has been increasingly used to analyse unknown substances and discover new elements.

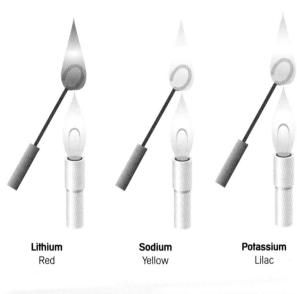

Lithium	Sodium	Potassium
Red	Yellow	Lilac

High energy level   Low energy level

Moving electrons

Chemical Patterns

Electron Configuration

Electron configuration tells you how the electrons are arranged around the **nucleus** of an **atom** in **shells**:

- The electrons in an atom occupy the lowest available shells (i.e. shells closest to the nucleus).
- The first shell can hold a maximum of 2 electrons.
- The shells after this can hold a maximum of 8 electrons.

Electron configuration is written as a series of numbers, e.g. 2.8.1. Going across a **period**, electron configuration increases by 1, e.g. sodium 2.8.1, magnesium 2.8.2, aluminium 2.8.3, until the outer shell is full, e.g. argon 2.8.8.

*N.B. This is only true for the first 20 **elements**.*

The electron configurations of the first 20 elements are shown below:

Electron Configuration of Fluorine (2.7)

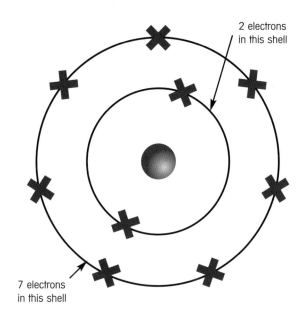

2 electrons in this shell

7 electrons in this shell

Hydrogen, H Atomic No. = 1	Helium, He Atomic No. = 2	Lithium, Li Atomic No. = 3	Beryllium, Be Atomic No. = 4	Boron, B Atomic No. = 5	Carbon, C Atomic No. = 6	Nitrogen, N Atomic No. = 7
1	2	2.1	2.2	2.3	2.4	2.5

Oxygen, O Atomic No. = 8	Fluorine, F Atomic No. = 9	Neon, Ne Atomic No. = 10	Sodium, Na Atomic No. = 11	Magnesium, Mg Atomic No. = 12	Aluminium, Al Atomic No. = 13	Silicon, Si Atomic No. = 14
2.6	2.7	2.8	2.8.1	2.8.2	2.8.3	2.8.4

Phosphorus, P Atomic No. = 15	Sulfur, S Atomic No. = 16	Chlorine, Cl Atomic No. = 17	Argon, Ar Atomic No. = 18	Potassium, K Atomic No. = 19	Calcium, Ca Atomic No. = 20
2.8.5	2.8.6	2.8.7	2.8.8	2.8.8.1	2.8.8.2

Key Words

Atom • Electron • Element • Nucleus • Period

HT Balanced Equations

The total mass of the **products** of a chemical reaction is always equal to the total mass of the **reactants**. This is because **no atoms are lost or made**.

So, chemical symbol equations must always be **balanced**. There must be the same number of atoms of each element on both sides of the equation.

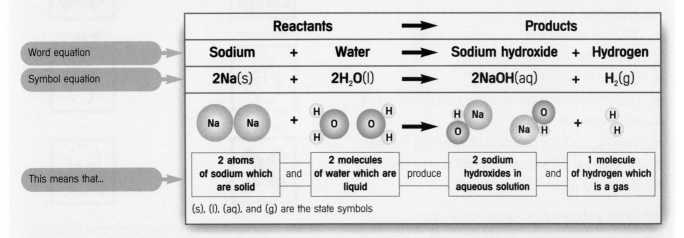

	Reactants	➡	Products	
Word equation	Sodium + Water	➡	Sodium hydroxide + Hydrogen	
Symbol equation	$2Na(s)$ + $2H_2O(l)$	➡	$2NaOH(aq)$ + $H_2(g)$	

This means that...

2 atoms of sodium which are solid	and	2 molecules of water which are liquid	produce	2 sodium hydroxides in aqueous solution	and	1 molecule of hydrogen which is a gas

(s), (l), (aq), and (g) are the state symbols

Writing Balanced Equations

Follow these steps to write a balanced equation:

1. Write a word equation for the chemical reaction.
2. Substitute in **formulae** for the elements or **compounds** involved.
3. Balance the equation by adding numbers in front of the reactants and/or products.
4. Write a balanced symbol equation.

	Reactants	➡	Products
1 Write a word equation	Magnesium + Oxygen	➡	Magnesium oxide
2 Substitute in formulae	Mg + O_2	➡	MgO

3 Balance the equation

- There are two **O**s on the reactant side, but only one **O** on the product side. We need to add another **MgO** to the product side to balance the **O**s.
- We now need to add another **Mg** on the reactant side to balance the **Mg**s.
- There are two magnesium atoms and two oxygen atoms on each side – it is **balanced**.

4 Write a balanced symbol equation

$2Mg(s)$ + $O_2(g)$ ➡ $2MgO(s)$

Chemical Patterns

Hazardous Substances

Hazards are identified by **symbols** that have specific meanings.

Common safety precautions for handling hazardous chemicals are as follows:

- Wearing gloves and eye protection, and washing hands after handling chemicals.
- Using safety screens.
- Using small amounts and low concentrations of the chemicals.
- Working in a fume cupboard or ventilating the room.
- Not eating or drinking when working with chemicals.
- Not working near naked flames.

Corrosive

Irritant

Flammable

Oxidising

Harmful

Toxic

Group 1 – The Alkali Metals

There are six metals in Group 1. The physical **properties** of the **alkali metals** alter as you go down the group. The further an **element** is down the group…

- the **higher** the **reactivity**
- the **lower** the **melting** and **boiling points**.

Group 1

Li
Lithium

Na
Sodium

K
Potassium

Element	Melting Point (°C)	Boiling Point (°C)	Density (g/cm³)
Lithium, Li	180	1340	0.53
Sodium, Na	98	883	0.97
Potassium, K	64	760	0.86
Rubidium, Rb	39	688	1.53
Caesium, Cs	29	671	1.90

HT Trends in Group 1

Alkali metals have similar properties because they all have **1 electron** in their outer shell.

The alkali metals become **more reactive** as you go down the group because the outer shell gets further away from the influence of the **nucleus** and so an electron is **more easily lost**.

Lithium Atom
2.1

Sodium Atom
2.8.1

Potassium Atom
2.8.8.1
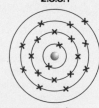

More reactive →

Key Words

Alkali metal • Compound • Element

Alkali Metal Compounds

Alkali metals can react to form **compounds**.

Alkali metals are shiny when freshly cut, but they quickly **tarnish in moist air**, go dull and become covered in a layer of metal oxide.

Alkali metals react **vigorously** with **chlorine** to form white crystalline **salts**.

A general equation can be used, where M refers to the alkali metal:

$$2M(s) + Cl_2(g) \longrightarrow 2MCl(s)$$

For example…

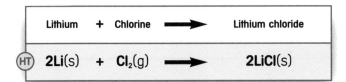

Alkali metals react with **water** to form a **metal hydroxide** and **hydrogen gas**. The metal hydroxide dissolves in water to form an **alkaline** solution:

$$2M(s) + 2H_2O(l) \longrightarrow 2MOH(aq) + H_2(g)$$

For example…

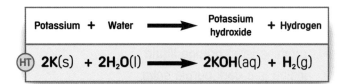

When lithium, sodium and potassium react with cold water they…
- **float** (due to their low density)
- **melt** because the heat from the reaction is great enough to turn them into liquids.

The reactivity of alkali metals increases further down the group:
- Lithium reacts gently.
- Sodium reacts more aggressively.
- Potassium reacts so aggressively it melts and catches fire.

Hazards of Alkali Metals

Alkali metals carry hazard symbols. When working with Group 1 metals, you should…
- use small amounts of very dilute concentrations
- wear safety glasses and use safety screens
- watch teacher demonstrations carefully
- avoid working near naked flames.

Chemical	Hazard Symbol	
Lithium	🔥	⚠️
Lithium chloride	✖	
Sodium	🔥	⚠️
Sodium hydroxide	⚠️	
Potassium	🔥	⚠️

Chemical Patterns

Group 7 – The Halogens

There are five non-metals in Group 7.

At room temperature and room pressure…
- chlorine is a **green gas**
- bromine is an **orange liquid**
- iodine is a **dark purple solid**.

All **halogens** consist of **diatomic molecules** (they only exist in pairs of **atoms**), e.g. Cl_2, Br_2, I_2.

You can use halogens to **bleach dyes** and **kill bacteria** in water. The physical **properties** of the halogens alter as you go down the group.

The further an element is down the group…
- the **lower** the **reactivity**
- the **higher** the **melting and boiling points**
- the **higher** the **density**.

Halogens react with alkali metals to produce **halides**.

Examples

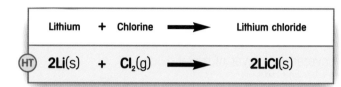

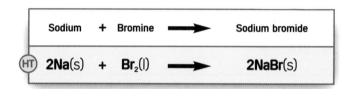

| Potassium | + | Iodine | ⟶ | Potassium iodide |
| **2K**(s) | + | I_2(s) | ⟶ | **2KI**(s) |

Element	Melting Point (°C)	Boiling Point (°C)	Density (g/cm³)
Fluorine, F_2	-220	-188	0.0016
Chlorine, Cl_2	-101	-34	0.003
Bromine, Br_2	-7	59	3.12
Iodine, I_2	114	184	4.95
Astatine, At_2	302 (estimated)	337 (estimated)	not known

HT Trends in Group 7

The halogens have similar properties because they all have **7 electrons** in their outer shell.

The halogens become **less reactive** as you go down the group because the outer shell gets further away from the influence of the **nucleus** and so an electron is **less easily gained**.

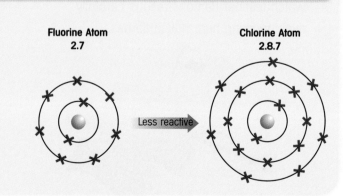

Hazards of Halogens

Halogens carry hazard symbols.

When working with halogens, you should…
- wear safety glasses
- work in a fume cupboard
- make sure the room is well ventilated
- use small amounts of very dilute concentrations
- avoid working near naked flames
- watch teacher demonstrations carefully.

Chemical	Hazard Symbol	
Fluorine, F	🔥	⚗
Chlorine, Cl	✕	
Bromine, Br	🔥	⚗

Displacement Reactions of Halogens

A **more reactive** halogen will **displace** a **less reactive** halogen from an aqueous solution of its salt. This means that chlorine will displace both bromine and iodine, while bromine will displace iodine.

Potassium iodide + Chlorine ➡ Potassium chloride + Iodine

(HT) $2KI(aq) + Cl_2(g) \longrightarrow 2KCl(aq) + I_2(aq)$

Halogen Compounds

Halogens can react to form **compounds**.

This table shows the compounds that are formed when halogens react with…
- Group 1 metals
- metal hydroxides (where M = metal).

	Chlorine	Bromine	Iodine
Lithium	LiCl	LiBr	LiI
Sodium	NaCl	NaBr	NaI
Potassium	KCl	KBr	KI
Metal hydroxide	MCl MClO	MBr MBrO	MI MIO

Properties of Compounds

Experiments show that **molten compounds** and aqueous solutions of metals with non-metals **conduct electricity**.

You can conclude from this that they are made up of **charged particles** called **ions**.

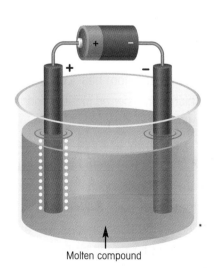

Molten compound

Key Words

Atom • Compound • Diatomic molecules • Displacement • Halogen • Ion

Chemical Patterns

Ions

Ions are **atoms** (or groups of atoms) that have **gained or lost electrons**.

As the **proton** and electron numbers are no longer equal, ions have an overall charge.

Sodium, Na Atom

Protons = 11
Electrons = 11

Equal number of protons and electrons, so no charge

Sodium, Na⁺ Ion

Protons = 11
Electrons = 10

1 more proton, so positive charge

Ionic Bonding

Ionic bonding occurs between a **metal** atom and a **non-metal** atom. Electrons transfer from one atom to another to form electrically charged ions:

- Atoms which **lose** electrons become **positively charged ions**.
- Atoms which **gain** electrons become **negatively charged ions**.

Each ion has a **full outer shell** of electrons.

Compounds of Group 1 metals and Group 7 **elements** are **ionic compounds (salts)**. Ionic compounds form **crystals** because the ions are arranged into a **regular lattice**. When ionic crystals melt or dissolve in water, they **conduct electricity**.

HT Ionic compounds conduct electricity when they are molten or dissolved in water, as the charged ions are free to move around the liquid.

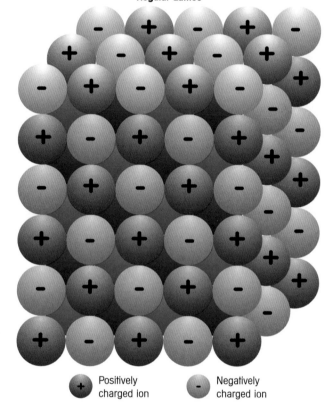

Regular Lattice

+ Positively charged ion

- Negatively charged ion

Example 1 – Sodium Chloride

Sodium and chlorine bond ionically to form sodium chloride, NaCl:

1. The sodium (Na) atom has 1 electron in its outer shell which is transferred to the chlorine (Cl) atom.
2. The sodium (Na) atom has lost 1 electron and is now a positively charged sodium ion (Na⁺) and the chlorine (Cl) atom has gained 1 electron and is now a negatively charged chlorine ion (Cl⁻).
3. Both atoms now have **8 electrons in their outer shell**. The atoms become ions Na⁺ and Cl⁻ and the compound formed is sodium chloride, NaCl.

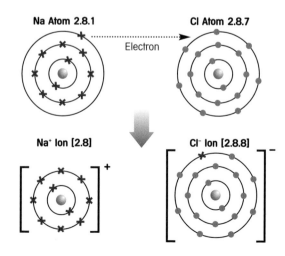

Na Atom 2.8.1   **Cl Atom 2.8.7**

Electron

Na⁺ Ion [2.8]   **Cl⁻ Ion [2.8.8]**

Chemical Patterns

Example 2 – Potassium Chloride

Potassium and chlorine bond ionically to form potassium chloride, KCl:

① The potassium (K) atom has 1 electron in its outer shell which is transferred to the chlorine (Cl) atom.

② The potassium (K) atom has lost 1 electron and is now a positively charged potassium ion (K^+) and the chlorine (Cl) atom has gained 1 electron and is now a negatively charged chlorine ion (Cl^-).

③ Both atoms now have **8 electrons in their outer shell**. The compound formed is potassium chloride, KCl.

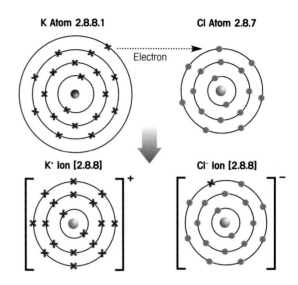

K Atom 2.8.8.1   Cl Atom 2.8.7
Electron
K^+ Ion [2.8.8] Cl^- Ion [2.8.8]

HT Formulae of Ionic Compounds

Ionic compounds are electrically **neutral** substances which have equal amounts of positive and negative charge.

If you know the charge given on both ions you can work out the formula.

For example, Na^+ and Cl^- combine to form NaCl.

If you know the formula and the charge on one of the ions, you can work out the charge on the other ion.

For example, $MgBr_2$ is made up of 2 lots of Br^- which combines with 1 lot of Mg^{2+}.

Positive Ions	Negative Ions	
	1– e.g. Cl^-, OH^-	2– e.g. SO_4^{2-}, O^{2-}
1+ e.g. K^+, Na^+	KCl 1+ 1–	K_2SO_4 2 x 1+ = 2+ 2–
	NaOH 1+ 1–	Na_2O 2 x 1+ = 2+ 2–
2+ e.g. Mg^{2+}, Cu^{2+}	$MgCl_2$ 2+ 2 x 1– = 2–	$MgSO_4$ 2+ 2–
	$Cu(OH)_2$ 2+ 2 x 1– = 2–	CuO 2+ 2–
3+ e.g. Al^{3+}, Fe^{3+}	$AlCl_3$ 3+ 3 x 1– = 3–	$Al_2(SO_4)_3$ 2 x 3+ = 6+ 3 x 2– = 6–
	$Fe(OH)_3$ 3+ 3 x 1– = 3–	Fe_2O_3 2 x 3+ = 6+ 3 x 2– = 6–

Key Words

Atom • Compound • Electron • Element • Ion • Ionic bond • Proton

Module C4 Summary

The Periodic Table

Element – made of only one kind of atom.

Elements are arranged in order of ascending proton number in the **periodic table**.

Group = vertical column of elements. Corresponds to the number of **electrons** in the outer shell of an atom.

Period = horizontal row of elements. Corresponds to the number of **shells** in an atom.

Atoms

Nucleus = made up of protons (positive) + neutrons (no charge).

Nucleus surrounded by electrons (negative) arranged in shells.

Atom has no overall charge.

Spectroscopy

Line spectrum = light emitted from flame of an element when heated.

Element	Colour of Flame
Lithium	Red
Sodium	Yellow
Potassium	Lilac

Electron Configuration

Electron configuration = how the electrons are arranged around nucleus.

First shell ➡ maximum of 2 electrons.

Shells after this ➡ maximum of 8 electrons.

Balanced Equations

Total mass of products = total mass of reactants.

No atoms are lost or made in a chemical reaction.

HT There are four steps to writing a balanced equation:
1. Write word equation.
2. Substitute in formulae.
3. Balance the equation by adding numbers in front of reactants / products.
4. Write balanced symbol equation.

Alkali Metals

Alkali metals ➡ Group 1 ➡ 1 electron in outer shell.

The reactivity of alkali metals **increases** down the group.

(HT) Alkali metals are **more reactive** down the group as the outer shell gets further from the nucleus and electrons are **more easily lost**.

Alkali metal + chlorine ➡ white crystalline salts.

Alkali metal + Water ⟶ Metal hydroxide + Hydrogen

Halogens

Halogens ➡ Group 7 ➡ 7 electrons in outer shell.

The reactivity of halogens **decreases** down the group.

At room temperature and room pressure…
- chlorine is a green gas
- bromine Is an orange liquid
- iodine is a dark purple solid.

(HT) Halogens are **less reactive** down the group as the outer shell gets further from the nucleus and electrons are **less easily gained**.

A more reactive halogen will **displace** a less reactive halogen from an aqueous solution of its salt.

Compounds

Ions = atoms that have gained or lost electrons so have an overall charge.

Ionic bonding = transfer of electrons between metals atoms and non-metals atoms.

Atom loses electrons ➡ positively charged ion.

Atom gains electrons ➡ negatively charged ion.

Ionic compound = compounds of Group 1 and Group 7 elements. Form **crystals** as ions are arranged in regular lattice.

When crystals melt or dissolve in water they conduct electricity.

(HT) Ionic compounds ➡ neutral substances ➡ equal amounts of positive and negative charge.

Module C4 Practice Questions

1. What do the group number and the period number tell us about the structure of an individual element?

....

....

2. Complete the table about atomic particles.

Atomic Particle	Relative Mass	Relative Charge
a)	1	**b)** ....
Neutron	**c)**	0
d)	Negligible	**e)** ....

3. Complete labels **A**, **B** and **C** for the diagram.

A ....

B ....

C ....

4. Match the following chemicals to the hazard labels that they carry. Each chemical may come under more than one hazard label.

Lithium   **Fluorine**   **Chlorine**   **Sodium hydroxide**

Corrosive: ....   Flammable: ....

Irritant: ....   Toxic: ....

5. **a)** What are halogens used for? ....

   b) List two precautions that should be taken when working with halogens.

   i) ....

   ii) ....

HT 6. The reactivity of the halogens decreases down the group, but the reactivity of the alkali metals increases down the group. Explain why there is this difference.

....

....

7 Sodium and chlorine react together to produce sodium chloride, NaCl.

a) Draw electron configuration diagrams for a sodium atom and a chlorine atom.

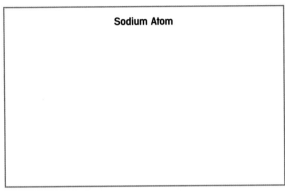

Sodium Atom

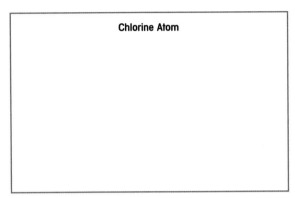

Chlorine Atom

b) Sodium chloride is an ionic compound. Explain how…

i) a sodium atom becomes a sodium ion _____

ii) a chlorine atom becomes a chlorine ion. _____

c) Draw an electron configuration diagram of sodium chloride.

Sodium Chloride

$$\Big[\qquad \Big] \qquad \qquad \Big[\qquad \qquad \Big]$$

Sodium Ion   Chlorine Ion

HT **8** Using the information below, predict the formula for the ionic compounds by completing the table.

Silver, Ag^+ Zinc, Zn^{2+} Aluminium, Al^{3+} Sulfate, SO_4^{2-}

Chloride, Cl^- Bromide, Br^- Nitrate, NO_3^-

Compound	Positive Ion	Negative Ion	Formula
Zinc bromide	Zn^{2+}	Br^-	$ZnBr_2$
Silver nitrate	a)	b)	$AgNO_3$
Aluminium chloride	c)	d)	e)
Aluminium sulfate	f)	g)	h)

Explaining Motion

Velocity

Velocity tells you an object's…
- speed
- direction of travel.

For example, if a lorry travels along a straight road at 15m/s (metres per second), in one direction, the velocity is +15m/s. If it then travels in the opposite direction, the velocity is -15m/s.

It doesn't matter which direction is called **positive** or **negative** as long as opposite directions have opposite signs.

This idea is also used when describing **distance**:
- Changes in distance in one direction are described as positive.
- In the opposite direction they're negative.

Calculating Speed

To calculate an object's speed you need to know…
- the **distance** it has travelled
- the **time** it took to travel that distance.

You can calculate speed using this formula:

$$\text{Speed (m/s)} = \frac{\text{Distance travelled (m)}}{\text{Time taken (s)}}$$

The formula calculates an **average speed** over the total distance travelled, even if the speed of an object isn't constant.

The speed of an object at a particular point in time is called the **instantaneous speed**.

Example

A car travels 10 metres in 5 seconds. What is its average speed?

$$\text{Speed} = \frac{\text{Distance Travelled}}{\text{Time Taken}} = \frac{10m}{5s} = \textbf{2m/s}$$

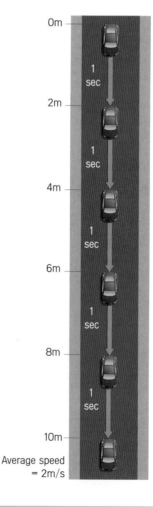

Average speed = 2m/s

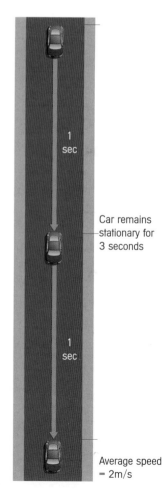

Car remains stationary for 3 seconds

Average speed = 2m/s

Explaining Motion

Distance–Time Graphs

The slope, or **gradient**, of a **distance–time graph** is a measure of the **speed** of the object. The **steeper the slope**, the **greater the speed**.

The graph shows the following:

1. A stationary person standing 15m away from point O.
2. A person moving at a constant speed.
3. A person moving at a greater constant speed.

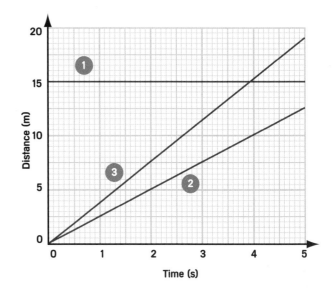

HT Calculating Speed

You can calculate the speed of an object by working out the gradient of a distance–time graph:

1. Take any two points on the gradient.
2. Read off the distance travelled between these points.
3. Note the time taken between these points.
4. Divide the distance by the time.

Speed from O to A = $\frac{15m}{3s}$ = **5m/s**

Speed from A to B = $\frac{15m - 15m}{5s}$ = **0m/s**

Speed from B to C = $\frac{15m}{4s}$ = **3.75m/s**

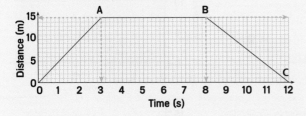

So, the object…
- travelled at 5m/s for 3 seconds
- remained stationary for 5 seconds
- then travelled at 3.75m/s for 4 seconds back to the starting point.

Remember…
- this calculation only works when looking at straight line sections
- the average velocity for this journey is 0 because the object ends up back where it started
- if you're asked to give velocity you need to indicate the direction. If the velocity in the first section is positive, the velocity in the last section will be negative because the object is moving in the opposite direction.

Key Words

Distance–time graph • Gradient • Instantaneous speed • Velocity

Explaining Motion

HT Curvy Distance–Time Graphs

When the line of a **distance–time graph** is curved, it means the **speed** of an object is **changing**:

- O to A – the line is curved. The object must be speeding up because the gradient is increasing.
- A to B – the line curves the other way. The object must be slowing down because the gradient is decreasing.

Because the graph is curved it's difficult to work out the **instantaneous speed**, but you can work out the average speed by dividing the total distance by the total time.

$$\text{Speed} = \frac{\text{Distance}}{\text{Time}}$$

$$= \frac{20\text{m}}{5\text{s}}$$

$$= \textbf{4m/s}$$

The dotted line shows the average speed. Where the gradient is…

- **steeper** than the dotted line, the object is travelling **faster** than the average speed
- **less steep** than the dotted line, the object is travelling **slower** than the average speed.

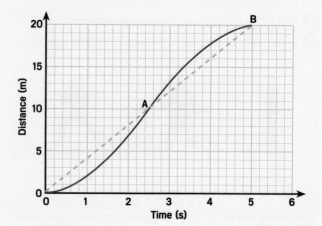

Velocity–Time Graphs

The slope, or gradient, of a **velocity–time graph** represents how quickly an object is increasing in speed (i.e. **accelerating**).

The steeper the slope, the faster its speed is increasing.

N.B. You need to be able to draw and interpret velocity–time graphs.

Velocity–time graphs are used in **lorry tachographs** to make sure that drivers…

- don't exceed the speed limit
- rest for suitable amounts of time.

Object is stationary.

 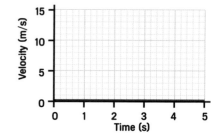

Object is moving at a constant speed.

Object is accelerating.

 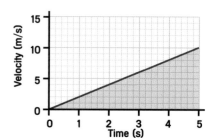

Key Words

Acceleration • Force • Friction • Gradient • Gravity • Velocity–time graph

Forces

A **force** occurs when two objects **interact** with each other.

Whenever one object exerts a force on another it always experiences a force in return.

The forces in an **interaction pair** are…
- **equal** in size
- **opposite** in direction.

Gravity (**weight**) – two masses are attracted to each other, e.g. you are attracted to the Earth and the Earth is attracted to you with an equal and opposite force.

Air resistance (drag) – the air tries to slow down a skydiver by pushing upwards against him / her. The skydiver pushes the air out of the way with an equal and opposite force.

Rocket and jet engines – the engine pushes gas backwards (action) and the gas pushes the rocket forwards (reaction).

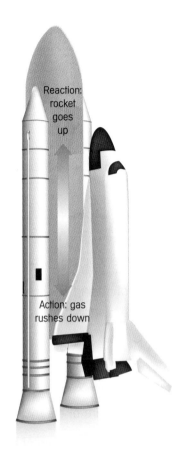

Reaction: rocket goes up

Action: gas rushes down

Friction and Reaction

Some forces only occur as a response to another force.

When an object is resting on a surface…
- the object is pulled down onto the surface by gravity
- the surface pushes up on the object with an equal force.

This is called the **reaction of the surface**.

When two objects try to slide past one another, both objects experience a force that tries to **stop them moving**.

This is called friction.

Objects don't have to be moving to experience friction. For example, the friction from a car's brakes stops it rolling down a hill.

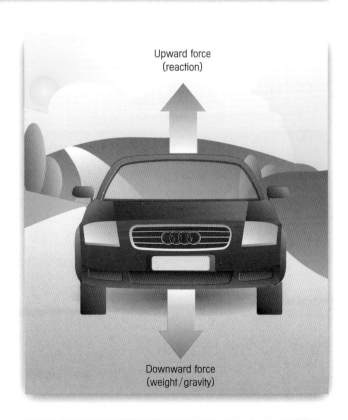

Upward force (reaction)

Downward force (weight / gravity)

Explaining Motion

Forces and Motion

Arrows are used when drawing diagrams of **forces**:
- The size of the arrow represents the size of the force.
- The direction of the arrow shows the direction it's acting in.

N.B. Force arrows are always drawn with the tail of the arrow touching the object even if the force is pushing the object.

If more than one force acts on an object they will…
- add up if they are acting in the same direction
- subtract if they are acting in opposite directions.

The overall effect of adding or subtracting these forces is called the **resultant force**.

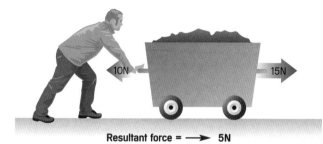

Resultant force = ⟶ 5N

Resultant force = ⟵ 15N

Momentum

Momentum is a measure of the motion of an object.

You can calculate the momentum of an object using this formula:

$$\text{Momentum (kg m/s)} = \text{Mass (kg)} \times \text{Velocity (m/s)}$$

$$\frac{p}{m \times v}$$

where p is momentum

If a car and a lorry are travelling at the same speed, the lorry will have more momentum because it has a bigger mass.

Example
A car has a mass of 1200kg and is travelling at a velocity of 30m/s. What is its momentum?

Momentum = Mass x Velocity
= 1200kg x 30m/s
= **36 000kg m/s**

Change in Momentum

If the **resultant force** acting on an object is zero, its momentum will not change, so, if the object is…
- stationary, it will remain stationary
- already moving, it will continue moving in a straight line at a steady speed.

If the resultant force acting on an object is not zero, it causes a change of momentum in the direction of the force. This could…
- make a stationary object move
- increase or decrease an object's speed
- change an object's direction.

The extent of the change in momentum depends on…
- the size of the resultant force
- the length of time the force is acting on the object.

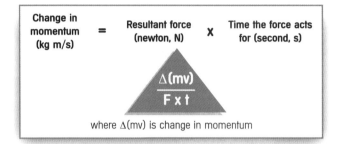

| Change in momentum (kg m/s) | = | Resultant force (newton, N) | x | Time the force acts for (second, s) |

$$\frac{\Delta(mv)}{F \times t}$$

where $\Delta(mv)$ is change in momentum

Collisions

Collisions cause changes in momentum.

For example, a car with a mass of 1000kg, travelling at 10m/s, has a momentum of 10 000kg m/s. If the car is involved in a collision and comes to a sudden stop, it would experience a change in momentum of 10 000kg m/s.

Sudden changes in momentum as a result of a collision can affect…
- the car
- the passengers – leading to injuries.

If the change in momentum is spread out over a longer period of time, the resultant force will be smaller.

Safety Devices

The force of the **impact** on the human body can be reduced by increasing the **time** of the impact.

This is the purpose of road safety devices, e.g.…
- seat-belts
- crumple zones – crumple on impact (e.g. motorcycle and bicycle helmets)
- air bags.

Crumple zone

Key Words

Force • Momentum • Resultant force

Explaining Motion

Speeding Up and Slowing Down

Cars and bicycles have a...

- **driving force** produced by the engine (car) or the energy of the cyclist (bicycle)
- **counter force** caused by friction and air resistance.

If the driving force is...

- **bigger than** the counter force, the vehicle speeds up
- **equal to** the counter force, the vehicle travels at a constant speed in a straight line
- **smaller than** the counter force, the vehicle slows down.

Car Speeds Up

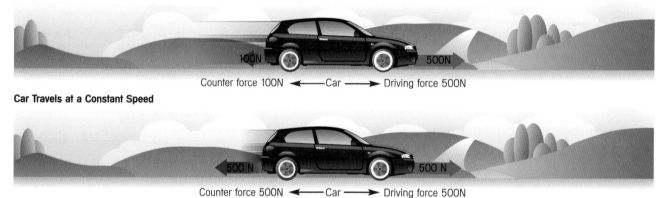

100N   500N

Counter force 100N ◄——Car——► Driving force 500N

Car Travels at a Constant Speed

500 N   500 N

Counter force 500N ◄——Car——► Driving force 500N

Car Slows Down.

1000N   500N

Counter force 1000N ◄——Car——► Driving force 500N

Kinetic Energy

A moving object has **kinetic energy**.

The amount of kinetic energy an object has depends on its...

- **mass**
- **velocity**.

The greater the mass and velocity of an object, the more kinetic energy it has. You can calculate kinetic energy using this formula:

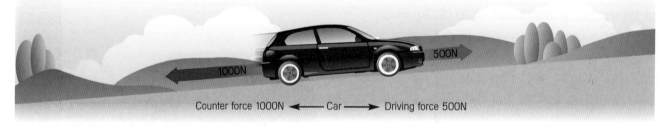

| Kinetic energy (joule, J) | = $\frac{1}{2}$ X | Mass (kilogram, kg) | X | Velocity^2 (metre per second, m/s)^2 |

KE
$\frac{1}{2}$ x m x v^2

Example

A bicycle of mass 50kg is moving at a velocity of 8m/s. How much kinetic energy does it have?

Kinetic energy = $\frac{1}{2}$ x Mass x Velocity^2

= $\frac{1}{2}$ x 50kg x (8m/s)^2

= $\frac{1}{2}$ x 50 x 64

= **1600J**

Work and Energy

Work is done by a force to move an object, resulting in the **transfer** of **energy**.

When work is done...
- **on** an object, the object **gains** energy
- **by** an object, the object **loses** energy.

The total amount of energy remains the same, i.e. energy is **conserved**.

> Change in Energy (joule, J) = Work done (joule, J)

When a force makes an object's velocity increase...
- work is done on the object
- the object gains kinetic energy.

If you ignore drag and friction, the increase in kinetic energy will be **equal to** the work done by the force. But, in reality, some of the energy will be dissipated (lost) as heat.

The relationship between work done, force and distance is shown by the formula:

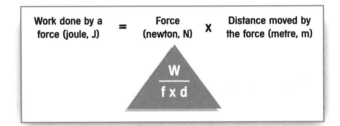

Gravitational Potential Energy

When an object is lifted above the ground...
- work is done by the lifting force against gravity
- the object has the potential to do work when it falls, e.g. a diver standing on a diving board.

This is called **gravitational potential energy** (GPE).

You can calculate change in GPE using this formula:

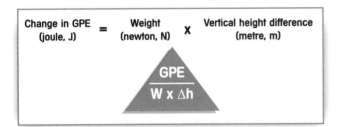

N.B. To find the GPE, you use the weight not the mass.

If an object is dropped, its GPE decreases and converts into kinetic energy.

Example

An object is dropped from a height of 5m. It has a mass of 2kg and weighs 20N. How much kinetic energy does it gain?

Change in GPE = Weight x Height difference
= 20N x 5m
= **100J**

The object...
- loses 100J of gravitational potential energy
- gains 100J of kinetic energy.

(HT) You can use the kinetic energy formula to work out the velocity of a falling object:

Kinetic energy = $\frac{1}{2}$ x Mass x V^2

$100 = \frac{1}{2}$ x 2 x V^2

$100 = V^2$

$V = \sqrt{100}$

= **10m/s**

Key Words

Force • Friction • Kinetic energy • Velocity

Module P4 Summary

Speed

Speed = how fast an object is moving.

Instantaneous speed = speed of an object at a particular point in time.

$$\text{Speed (m/s)} = \frac{\text{Distance travelled (m)}}{\text{Time taken (s)}}$$

Distance–Time Graphs

The **gradient** of a distance–time graph represents the **speed** of an object.

Steeper the slope ➡ **greater** the speed.

(HT) To calculate speed using a distance–time graph:
1. Take any two points on the gradient.
2. Read off the distance travelled between these points.
3. Note the time taken between these points.
4. Divide the distance by the time.

Curvy distance time graphs = speed of an object is changing.

Average speed of a curvy distance–time graph = total distance divided by total time.

Gradient steeper than dotted line ➡ object travelling faster than average speed.

Gradient less steep than dotted line ➡ object travelling slower than average speed.

Velocity

Velocity = describes an object's speed and direction.

The **gradient** of a velocity–time graph represents how quickly an object is increasing in speed.

Steeper the slope ➡ **faster** the speed is increasing.

Velocity–time graphs are used in **lorry tachographs** to make sure that drivers get rest and don't exceed speed limits.

Forces

Force – occurs when two objects interact with each other.

Forces in an interaction pair are...
- equal in size
- opposite in direction.

Gravity = force of attraction between all masses.

Air resistance = air tries to slow an object down.

Reaction of the surface = an object is pulled down onto the surface by gravity and the surface pushes up onto the object with an equal force.

Friction = the force that tries to stop two objects moving as they slide past one another.

Resultant force = overall effect of adding or subtracting forces.

Size of force arrow = size of force.

Direction of force arrow = direction force is acting in.

Force arrows are always drawn with the tail of the arrow touching the object.

Momentum

Momentum = measure of the motion of an object.

$$\text{Momentum (kg m/s)} = \text{Mass (kg)} \times \text{Velocity (m/s)}$$

$$\text{Change in momentum (kg m/s)} = \text{Resultant force (newton, N)} \times \text{Time the force acts for (second, s)}$$

Collisions – cause changes in momentum.

If a change in momentum is **spread out** over a longer period of time, the resultant force will be **smaller**.

Increasing **time** of impact ➡ reduces **force** of impact.

Energy

Kinetic energy = the energy an object has because of its movement. It depends on the mass and velocity of an object.

$$\text{Kinetic energy (joule, J)} = \frac{1}{2} \times \text{Mass (kilogram, kg)} \times \text{Velocity}^2 \text{ (metre per second, m/s)}^2$$

Work is done by a force to move an object, resulting in the **transfer** of energy.

Work done **on** an object ➡ object **gains** energy.

Work done **by** an object ➡ object **loses** energy.

$$\text{Work done by a force (joule, J)} = \text{Force (newton, N)} \times \text{Distance moved by the force (metre, m)}$$

Change in energy = work done.

Gravitational potential energy = energy an object has because of its mass and height above the Earth.

Object is dropped ➡ GPE decreases ➡ kinetic energy increases.

$$\text{Change in GPE (joule, J)} = \text{Weight (newton, N)} \times \text{Vertical height difference (metre, m)}$$

Module P4 Practice Questions

1. Name two things that velocity tells you about an object.

   a) .... b) ....

2. A bus travels 20 metres in 5 seconds. What is its average speed?

   ....

   ....

3. What is instantaneous speed?

   ....

4. a) The graph shows three different journeys. Match statements **A**, **B** and **C** with the labels **1–3** on the graph.

   A The person is moving at the fastest speed. ◯

   B The person is moving at the slowest speed. ◯

   C The person is stationary. ◯

   HT b) Using the graph above, calculate the average speed of journey three.

   ....

5. Explain why velocity–time graphs are used in lorry tachographs.

   ....

6. What is friction?

   ....

   ....

7. Use the words from the list below, to complete the following paragraph.

   add up　　　　**resultant force**　　　　**momentum**　　　　**subtract**　　　　**velocity**

   If two forces are acting on an object in the same direction they will .... If they are

   acting on an object in opposite directions they will .... The overall effect is called

   the ....

8 Calculate the momentum of a car that has a mass of 1500kg and is travelling at a velocity of 45m/s.

....

....

9 a) Name three road safety devices.

i) .... ii) .... iii) ....

b) Explain how safety devices reduce the force of impact on the human body.

....

10 If the driving force of a car is bigger than the counter force, what will happen to the car? Tick the correct option.

A The car will stop. ◯ **B** The car will slow down. ◯

C The car will speed up. ◯ **D** The car will travel at a constant speed. ◯

11 A lorry of mass 1200kg is moving at a velocity of 12m/s. How much kinetic energy does it have?

....

....

12 If work is done by a force to move an object, what happens to the total amount of energy?

....

13 A ball is dropped from a height of 8m. It has a mass of 2kg and weighs 18N.

a) Calculate how much kinetic energy the ball gains as it falls.

....

....

b) How much gravitational potential energy does the ball lose?

....

HT **c)** Calculate the velocity of the falling ball just before it hits the ground.

....

....

Growth and Development

Cells

Cells are the building blocks of all living things.

All cells contain...

- **DNA**
- **organelles**.

DNA molecules are in the form of a **double helix** and contain the genetic code.

Organelles are the different parts of the cell's structure. They do different jobs within the cell and work together to allow the cell to perform a specific function.

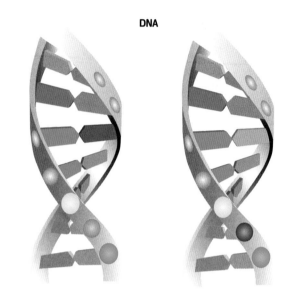

DNA

Animal Cells

Human cells, most animal cells and plant cells have the following parts:

- **Cytoplasm** – where most chemical reactions take place.
- **Nucleus** – contains genetic information.
- **Ribosomes** – where protein synthesis takes place.
- A **cell membrane** – controls movement into and out of the cell.

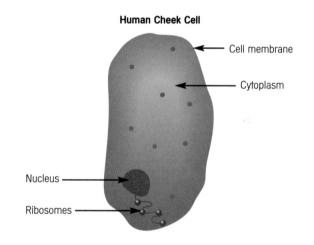

Human Cheek Cell

Cell membrane

Cytoplasm

Nucleus

Ribosomes

Plant Cells

Plant cells also have the following parts:

- A **cell wall** – strengthens the cell.
- A **permanent vacuole** – helps support the cell.
- **Chloroplasts** – absorb light energy to make food.

Key Words

Chromosome • DNA • Gamete • Meiosis • Mitosis • Nucleus • Organelles • Ribosome

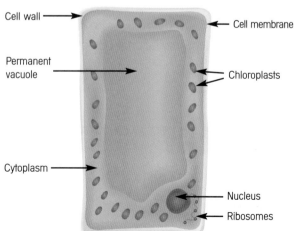

Plant Cell

Cell wall

Cell membrane

Permanent vacuole

Chloroplasts

Cytoplasm

Nucleus

Ribosomes

Growth and Development

Mitosis

Mitosis is the division of body cells to produce new cells. Each new cell has…

- **identical** sets of **chromosomes** as the parent cell
- the **same number** of chromosomes as the parent cell
- the same genes as the parent cell.

Mitosis occurs…
- for growth
- for repair
- to replace old tissues.

To enable mitosis to take place, cells go through a cycle of **growth** and then **division**. The cycle repeats itself until the cell can no longer divide.

When a cell enters the **growth phase** of the cycle…
- the number of **organelles increase**
- the **chromosomes** are **copied** – the two strands of each DNA molecule separate and new strands form alongside them.

When a cell enters the **division phase** of the cycle…
- the copies of the **chromosomes separate**
- the cell **divides**.

Parent cell with two pairs of chromosomes.

Each chromosome copies itself.

The copies are pulled apart. Cell now divides for the only time in this mitosis sequence.

Two 'daughter' cells are formed.

Meiosis

Meiosis only takes place in the **testes** and **ovaries** and is a special type of cell division which produces **gametes** (egg and sperm) for sexual reproduction.

Gametes contain **half** the number of chromosomes as the parent cell.

| Cell with two pairs of chromosomes. | Each chromosome replicates itself. | Chromosomes part company and move to opposite sides with their 'copies'. | Cell divides for the first time. | Copies now separate and the second cell division takes place. | Four gametes, each with half the number of chromosomes of the parent cell. |

Growth and Development

Fertilisation

During **fertilisation**, a **male gamete** (sperm) and a **female gamete** (egg) fuse together to produce a single body cell, called a **zygote**.

Gametes only have half the number of **chromosomes** as the parent cell, so the zygote that's produced has **one whole set** of chromosomes.

In each new pair of chromosomes…
* one chromosome comes from the father
* one chromosome comes from the mother.

The zygote then divides by **mitosis** to produce a cluster of cells called an **embryo**.

The embryo continues to develop by mitosis (from one cell to two, to four, to eight, etc.) to eventually become an adult individual.

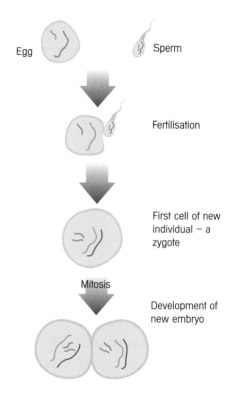

Egg · Sperm

Fertilisation

First cell of new individual – a zygote

Mitosis

Development of new embryo

Variation

Meiosis and **sexual reproduction** produce **variation** between offspring and parents:
* When the gametes fuse, genetic information from two individuals is combined.
* For each gene, just one of each parent's alleles is passed on.
* Each offspring can have a different combination of alleles from either parent.
* The offspring have different characteristics from each other

Genes

Genes are present on the **chromosomes** in each cell **nucleus**.

Genes control…
* growth and development in organisms
* the development of characteristics, e.g. eye colour.

Key Words

Chromosome • Embryo • Fertilisation • Gamete • Gene • Meiosis • Mitosis • Nucleus • Ribosome • Zygote

Genetic Code

Genes control **characteristics** by providing instructions for the production of **proteins**.

The instructions are in the form of a **code**, made up of **four bases** which hold the two strands of the **DNA molecule** together. These bases always pair up in the same way:

- Adenine (A) pairs with thymine (T).
- Cytosine (C) pairs with guanine (G).

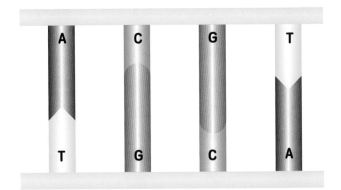

Controlling Growth and Development

DNA is **too large** to leave the nucleus. The genes therefore stay inside the nucleus but the production of proteins takes place **outside** the nucleus, in the **cytoplasm**.

Information stored in the genes has to be transferred into the cytoplasm.

This transfer is done in the following way:

1. The relevant section of DNA is unzipped.
2. Instructions are copied onto smaller molecules called **messenger RNA (mRNA)**.
3. The mRNA leave the nucleus and carry the instructions to the **ribosomes**.
4. The ribosomes follow the instructions to make the relevant protein.

HT The sequence of bases in a gene determines the order in which **amino acids** are joined together to make a particular **protein**.

A group of **three** base pairs codes for one amino acid in a protein chain, called a **triplet code**. There are 20 different amino acids that can be made.

The structure of the protein depends on the amino acids that make it up.

This process is as follows:

1. DNA unravels at the correct gene.
2. A copy of the coding strand is made to produce mRNA.
3. The mRNA copy moves from the nucleus into the cytoplasm.
4. The triplet code is decoded by the ribosomes.
5. Amino acids are joined together to form a polypeptide (protein).

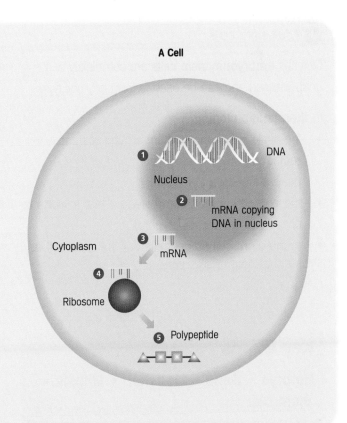

A Cell

Growth and Development

Development of New Organisms

Up to the eight cell stage, all cells in a human **embryo**…
- are unspecialised
- can turn into **any** kind of cell.

These cells are known as **embryonic stem cells**.

After the eight cell stage, the cells in an embryo…
- become **specialised**
- form different types of **tissue**.

The cells contain the **same genes**, but many genes are **not active** because the cell only produces the **proteins** it needs to carry out its role.

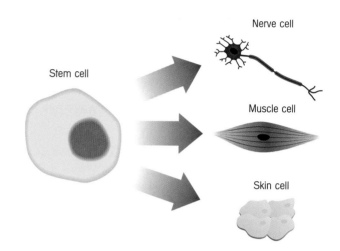

HT Stem Cells

Stem cells could potentially be used to…
- help treat diseases and disorders
- repair damage to various tissues.

There are three sources of stem cells:
1. Embryos.
2. Blood from the umbilical cord.
3. Adult stem cells.

Only the **embryonic stem cells** are completely unspecialised and can be used to form any cell type.

In **therapeutic cloning**…
- the nucleus is removed from an egg cell and replaced with a nucleus from one of the patient's cells
- the egg cell is then stimulated so that it starts to divide (as if it were a zygote)
- at the eight cell stage, cells can be removed as they are still unspecialised.

Adult stem cells will only produce cells of a certain type. For example, cells for creating blood cells in bone marrow have to be encouraged to grow more of that type of cell by reactivating (switching back on) inactive genes in the nuclei.

The advantage of using adult cells for growing replacement tissue is that they can be taken from the patient, so the patient's immune system will not reject the transplant.

Replacement tissue can either be grown in a laboratory, or by using a 'host animal' (e.g. a mouse) to maintain a blood supply during growth.

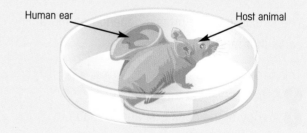

Key Words

Embryo • Gene • Meristem • Mitosis • Stem cell

Differentiation in Plants

Plant cells divide by the process of **mitosis**.

New cells in plants specialise into the cells of…
- roots
- leaves
- flowers.

Unlike animals, most plants continue to grow in **height** and **width** throughout their lives.

Meristems

Plant growth occurs in areas called **meristems**, which are sites where **unspecialised cells** divide repeatedly.

These cells then…
- differentiate
- become specialised.

There are **two types** of meristems:
- **Lateral** which leads to increased girth.
- **Apical** which leads to increased height and longer roots.

Some plant cells remain **unspecialised** and can develop into any type of plant cell. These cells allow **clones** of plants with desirable features to be produced from **cuttings**.

If the **hormonal conditions** in their environment are changed, the unspecialised plant cells can develop into other…
- **tissues**, e.g. xylem and phloem
- **organs**, e.g. leaves, roots and flowers.

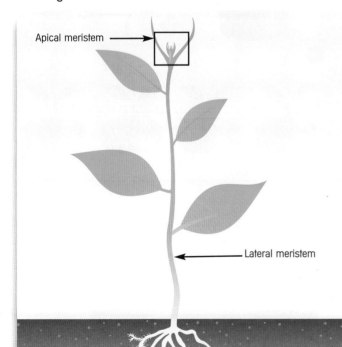

Apical meristem

Lateral meristem

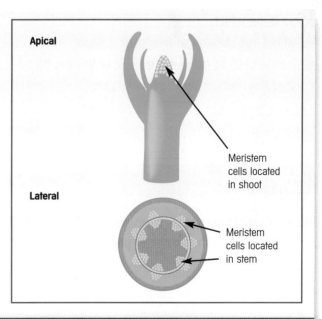

Apical

Lateral

Meristem cells located in shoot

Meristem cells located in stem

Growth and Development

Xylem and Phloem

Xylem tubes are used by the plant to…
- transport water and soluble mineral salts from the roots to the stem and leaves
- replace water lost during transpiration and photosynthesis.

Phloem tubes are used by the plant to transport dissolved food to the whole plant for respiration or storage.

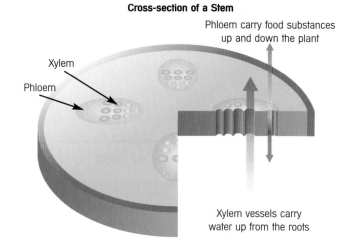

Cross-section of a Stem

Phloem carry food substances up and down the plant

Xylem

Phloem

Xylem vessels carry water up from the roots

Cuttings

Plants can be reproduced in the following way:
1. Cuttings are taken from a plant.
2. The cuttings are put in a rooting hormone.
3. Roots start to form and the new plants develop.

The new plants are **genetically identical** to the parent plant, i.e. they are **clones**.

(HT) **Auxins** are the main plant hormones used in horticulture, which…
- affect cell division at the tip of a shoot
- cause cells to grow in size just under the tip so that the stem or roots grow longer.

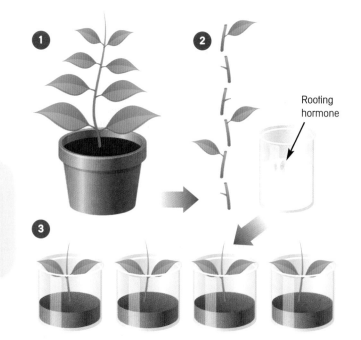

Rooting hormone

Phototropism

Plants respond to light by changing the direction in which they grow. This is called **phototropism**.

They grow towards a light source as they need light to survive.

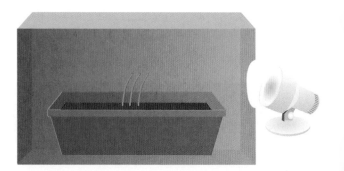

Key Words

Auxin • Clone • Phototropism

HT How Phototropism Works

Auxin is produced at the shoot tip. It moves down the shoot, causing cells further down the shoot to grow.

When light shines on a shoot, auxin moves away from the light source.

This causes the cells furthest away from the light to lengthen, so the shoot bends towards the light source.

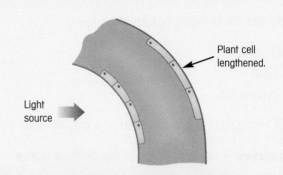

Plant cell lengthened.

Light source

---

1 When a light source is directly overhead…
- auxin is evenly spread through the shoot
- the shoot grows **straight** up.

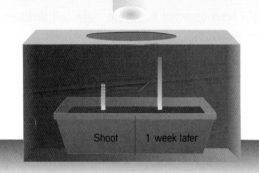

Shoot | 1 week later

---

2 When a light source is at an angle…
- auxin moves away from the light source
- the auxin is concentrated on the side furthest away from the light
- the shoot **bends** towards the light.

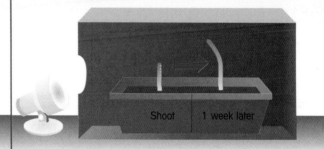

Shoot | 1 week later

---

3 If the tip of the shoot is removed or covered in opaque material then the plant will continue to grow upwards – as if the light source was not there.

Opaque cap

Shoot | 1 week later

---

4 If the tip is covered with a transparent cap then it will still grow towards the light source. The same thing will happen if an opaque cylinder is wrapped around the stem leaving the tip exposed.

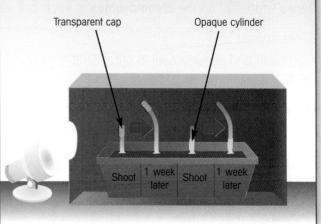

Transparent cap | Opaque cylinder

Shoot | 1 week later | Shoot | 1 week later

Module B5 Summary

Cells

Cells are the building blocks of all living things.

Cells contain…
- DNA
- organelles.

DNA molecules are in the form of a double helix and contain the genetic code.

Organelles = different parts of the cell's structure.

Animal and plants cells have cytoplasm, a nucleus, ribosomes and a cell membrane.

Plant cells also have a cell wall, a permanent vacuole and chloroplasts.

Cell Division

Mitosis = division of body cells to produce new cells. Each new cell contains the same genetic information as the parent cell.

Organelles increase ➡ chromosomes copied ➡ copies of chromosomes separate ➡ cell divides.

Meiosis = division of cells in the testes and ovaries to produce gametes for sexual reproduction.

Gametes – contain half the number of chromosomes as the parent cell.

Fertilisation

During **fertilisation**, a male gamete and a female gamete fuse together to produce a **zygote**.

Zygote – has one whole set of chromosomes.

After fertilisation, the zygote divides by mitosis to produce an **embryo**.

Genes

Genes – present on the **chromosomes** in each cell nucleus.

Genes control…
- growth and development in organisms
- development of characteristics.

Meiosis and sexual reproduction produce **variation** between offspring and parents as genetic information from two individuals is combined.

Genetic code – made up of four bases which hold the two strands of the **DNA molecule** together.

Bases always pair up in the same way:
- Adenine with thymine.
- Cytosine with guanine.

mRNA = small molecules which leave the nucleus and carry genetic information into the cytoplasm.

Ribosomes – follow instructions from the mRNA to make proteins.

(HT) A group of three base pairs codes for one amino acid in a protein chain, called a triplet code. There are 20 different amino acids that can be made.

Stem Cells

Embryonic stem cells – unspecialised cells that can turn into any kind of cell.

After the eight cell stage, the cells in an embryo become specialised and can form different types of tissue.

(HT) Stem cells can be used to treat diseases and disorders and repair damage to various tissues.

The three sources of stem cells are embryos, blood from the umbilical cord and adult stem cells.

Plant Growth

New cells in plants specialise into the cells of…
- roots
- leaves
- flowers.

Meristem = area of plant growth, where unspecialised cells divide repeatedly.

Lateral meristem = leads to increased girth.

Apical meristem = leads to increased height and longer roots.

Xylem tubes = transport **water** from the roots to the stem and leaves and replace lost water.

Phloem tubes = transport **dissolved food** to the whole plant for respiration or storage.

Plant Cuttings

New plants develop when cuttings are taken from a plant and put in a rooting hormone. The new plants are clones of the parent plant.

(HT) **Auxins** = main plant hormones used in horticulture which cause cell growth and division.

Phototropism

Phototropism = growth of plants towards a light source.

(HT) Light source overhead ➡ auxin spread evenly ➡ shoot grows straight up.

Light source at an angle ➡ auxin on side furthest from light ➡ shoot bends towards light.

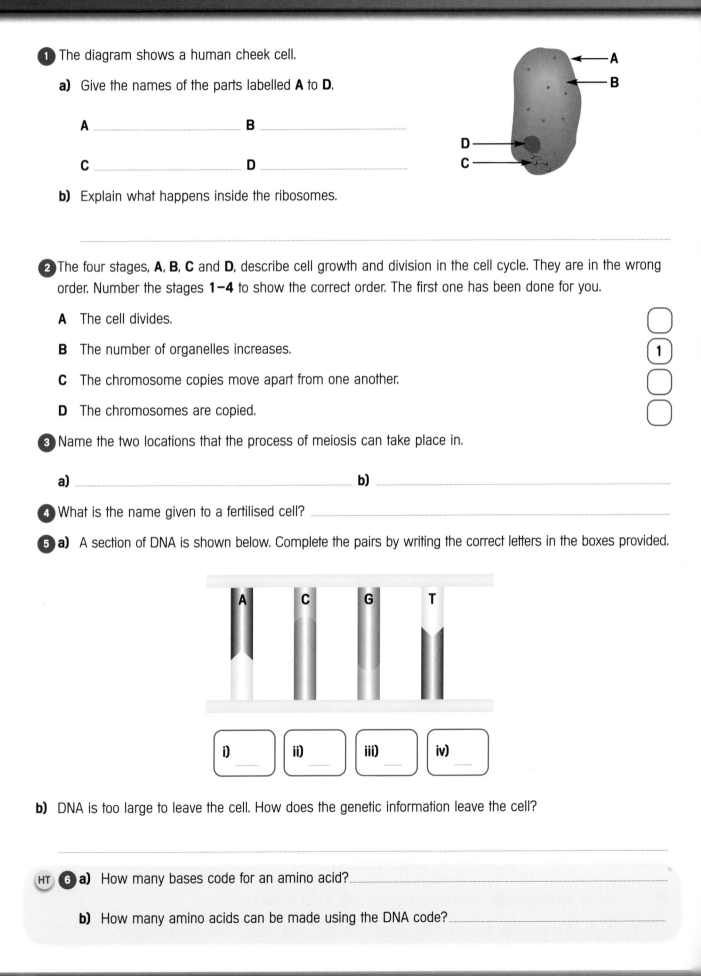

1 The diagram shows a human cheek cell.

a) Give the names of the parts labelled **A** to **D**.

A .... B ....

C .... D ....

b) Explain what happens inside the ribosomes.

....

2 The four stages, **A**, **B**, **C** and **D**, describe cell growth and division in the cell cycle. They are in the wrong order. Number the stages **1–4** to show the correct order. The first one has been done for you.

A The cell divides.

B The number of organelles increases.

C The chromosome copies move apart from one another.

D The chromosomes are copied.

1

3 Name the two locations that the process of meiosis can take place in.

a) .... b) ....

4 What is the name given to a fertilised cell? ....

5 a) A section of DNA is shown below. Complete the pairs by writing the correct letters in the boxes provided.

A   C   G   T

i) ....   ii) ....   iii) ....   iv) ....

b) DNA is too large to leave the cell. How does the genetic information leave the cell?

....

HT **6** a) How many bases code for an amino acid? ....

b) How many amino acids can be made using the DNA code? ....

7 a) What are the characteristics of stem cells?

....

b) Why can't stem cells be taken after the eight cell stage?

....

8 Fill in the missing word to complete the sentence below:

Plant growth occurs in parts of the plant called ....

9 Describe the roles of the following:

a) Phloem tubes ....

b) Xylem tubes ....

10 Naveen is experimenting with plant shoots and light. She takes a plant shoot and shines light onto it from one side (shown in the diagram below).

a) Draw how the plant shoot would look after 12 hours.

HT b) On the plant shoot that you have drawn in part **a)**, add the letter A to show where the plant growth hormone auxin is produced.

c) On what side of the plant shoot will most of the auxin be found?

....

11 What does auxin do to cells?

....

Chemicals of the Natural Environment

The Earth's Resources

The Earth is made up of different parts.

The **atmosphere** is a layer of gas surrounding the Earth. It is made up of the **elements** nitrogen, oxygen and argon, some **compounds** (e.g. carbon dioxide) and water vapour.

The **hydrosphere** is mostly made up of water and some dissolved compounds.

The **biosphere** is made up of all the living organisms on Earth. They are all made up of compounds containing the elements carbon, hydrogen, oxygen and nitrogen and small amounts of phosphorus and sulfur.

The **lithosphere** is the rigid outer layer of the Earth, made up of the crust and the part of the mantle just below it. It consists of a mixture of minerals (e.g. silicon dioxide), and an abundance of the elements silicon, oxygen and aluminium.

Chemical Cycles

Chemicals constantly move between the different spheres in cycles. Life depends on this movement of chemicals.

The following are examples of chemical cycles:
- The oxygen cycle.
- The carbon cycle.
- The nitrogen cycle.

The flow chart shows the nitrogen cycle.

N.B. You need to be able to interpret flow charts like this.

The Nitrogen Cycle

Atmosphere Contains N_2

Denitrifying bacteria

Biosphere Plant – proteins

Eaten

Biosphere Animal

Death of animals and excretion

Taken up by roots

Death

Lithosphere Nitrates in soil (NO_3)

Lightning storms

Nitrogen-fixing bacteria

Making and using fertilisers

Ammonium products

Nitrifying bacteria in soil

Lithosphere NH_4

Key Words

Atmosphere • Biosphere • Compound • Element • Hydrosphere • Lithosphere

Chemicals of the Atmosphere

The chemicals that make up the atmosphere consist of…

- non-metal elements
- molecular compounds made up from non-metal elements.

From the table you can see that the molecules (with the exception of water) that make up the atmosphere are gases at 20°C because they have **low boiling points**. This can be explained by looking at the structure of the molecules:

- Gases have small molecules with weak forces of attraction between them.
- Only small amounts of energy are needed to break these forces, which allows the molecules to move freely through the air.

Pure molecular compounds don't conduct electricity because their molecules aren't charged.

HT The atoms within molecules are connected by strong **covalent bonds**. In a covalent bond…

- the **electrons** are shared between the **atoms**.
- a strong, **electrostatic attraction** is caused between the positive nuclei and shared pair of negative electrons.

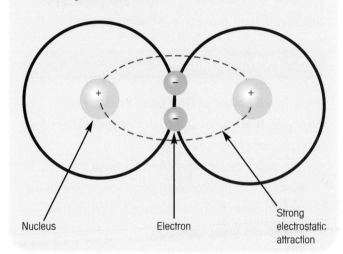

Nucleus   Electron   Strong electrostatic attraction

Chemical	2-D Molecular Diagram	3-D Molecular Diagram	Boiling Point (°C)	Melting Point (°C)
Oxygen O_2	O=O		−182.9	−218.3
Nitrogen N_2	N≡N		−195.8	−210.1
Carbon dioxide CO_2	O=C=O		−78	Sublimes (no liquid state)
Water vapour H_2O	H−O−H		100	0
Argon Ar	Ar		−185.8	−189.3

Chemicals of the Natural Environment

Chemicals of the Hydrosphere

Sea water in the **hydrosphere** is 'salty' because it contains dissolved **ionic compounds** called **salts**.

For example, sodium chloride is an ionic compound made from positive sodium **ions** and negative chlorine ions. The ions are **electrostatically attracted** to each other to form a **3-D giant crystal lattice** with high melting and boiling points.

HT When given a table of charges on **ions**, you need to be able to work out the **formulae for salts** in the sea.

For example, you should be able to work out the formulae for sodium chloride, magnesium sulfate, potassium chloride and potassium bromide.

The Water Molecule

Water has a **higher boiling point** than the other molecules that make up the **atmosphere**. This can be explained by its structure:

- The water molecule is bent, because the **electrons** in the **covalent bond** are nearer to the oxygen **atom** than the hydrogen atoms. This makes it a **polar molecule**.
- The small charges on the atoms mean that the forces between the molecules are **stronger** than in other covalent molecules so more energy is needed to separate them.

Polar Water Molecule

Slight negative charge

Oxygen atom

Shared electrons are nearer the oxygen atom than the hydrogen atoms

Hydrogen atom

Slight positive charge

Dissolving Ionic Compounds

The small charges on water molecules help them to dissolve **ionic compounds**:

1. A water molecule is attracted to an ion in the crystal lattice.
2. An ion breaks away from the lattice.
3. The ion moves freely through the water.

Ionic compounds **conduct electricity** when dissolved in water because the ions are charged and are able to move freely through the water.

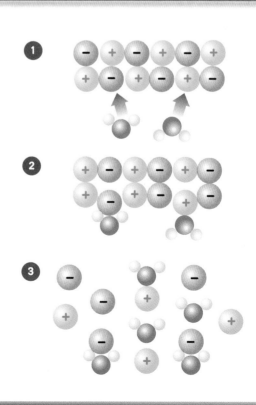

Key Words

Atmosphere • Atom • Compound • Covalent bond • Element • Electron • Hydrosphere • Ion

Chemicals of the Natural Environment

Chemicals of the Lithosphere

This table shows the abundance of **elements** in the Earth's crust (lithosphere). For example, you can see that the three most abundant elements are…

- oxygen
- silicon
- aluminium.

N.B. You may be asked to interpret data like this in your exam.

A lot of the silicon and oxygen in the Earth's crust is present as the compound **silicon dioxide** (SiO_2).

Silicon dioxide forms a **giant covalent structure**:
- Each silicon atom is covalently bonded to four oxygen atoms.
- Each oxygen atom is bonded to two silicon atoms.

Element	Abundance in Lithosphere (ppm)
Oxygen, O	455 000
Silicon, Si	272 000
Aluminium, Al	83 000
Iron, Fe	62 000
Calcium, Ca	46 600
Magnesium, Mg	27 640
Sodium, Na	22 700
Potassium, K	18 400
Titanium, Ti	6 320
Hydrogen, H	1 520

Properties of Silicon Dioxide

Silicon dioxide has the following properties:
- **Hard**, **high melting point**, **high boiling point** − as its strong, rigid 3-dimensional structure is very difficult to break down.
- **Electrical insulator** − as there are no ions or free electrons.
- **Insoluble in water** − as there are no charges to attract water molecules.

Silicon dioxide is found as **quartz** in granite, and is the main constituent of sandstone.

Some forms of quartz are used as **gemstones**, which can be very valuable because of their rarity, hardness and shiny appearance.

HT By understanding giant covalent structures, you can explain why different materials are used for certain jobs. This table gives some examples.

Element/Compound	Property	Use	Explanation
Carbon − diamond	Very hard	Drill tips	A lot of energy is needed to break the strong covalent bonds between the atoms.
Silicon dioxide	High melting point (1610℃)	Furnace linings	A lot of energy is needed to break the strong covalent bonds between the atoms.
Silica glass	Doesn't conduct electricity	Insulator in electrical devices	No free electrons or ions to carry electrical charge.

Chemicals of the Natural Environment

Chemicals of the Biosphere

The **biosphere** contains three important groups of molecules:

- Carbohydrates.
- Proteins.
- **DNA.**

Carbohydrates (for example, glucose) contain…

- carbon
- oxygen
- hydrogen.

Proteins are polymers made from amino acid monomers joined together. One of the simplest amino acids is glycine.

DNA is a large complex molecule.

*N.B. From a diagram of a molecule, you need to be able to identify the **elements** in the compound and write its formula.*

The table below lists the **percentage composition** of carbohydrates, proteins, fats and DNA.

N.B. You need to be able to interpret this type of data.

For example, from the table you can see that…

- Protein 2 contains more carbon than Protein 1
- DNA is the only molecule to contain phosphorus.

Glucose, $C_6H_{12}O_6$

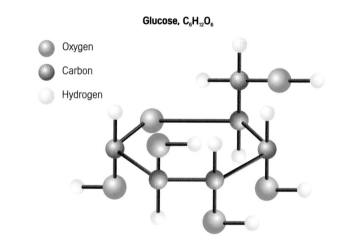

Glycine, $NH_2CH_2CO_2H$

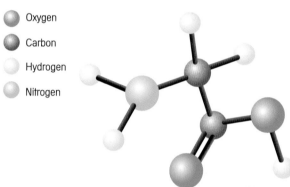

DNA Molecule

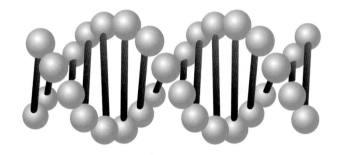

	Carbon %	Oxygen %	Hydrogen %	Nitrogen %	Phosphorus %
Carbohydrate	40.0	53.3	6.7	0	0
Protein 1	32.0	42.7	6.7	18.7	0
Protein 2	40.4	36.0	7.9	15.7	0
Fat	39.0	52.0	8.7	0	0
DNA	41.0	30.7	4.6	29.0	4.2

Chemicals of the Natural Environment

Balancing Equations

In all chemical reactions, the mass of the **reactants** is **equal** to the mass of the **products**.

If you need to balance an equation, follow this method:

1 Write a number in front of one or more of the formulae to balance each element.

2 Include the state symbols:

- (s) solid
- (l) liquid
- (g) gas
- (aq) dissolved in water (aqueous solution).

Balancing Equations – Example

Balance the reaction between calcium carbonate and hydrochloric acid.

Calcium carbonate	+	Hydrochloric acid	⟶	Calcium chloride	+	Carbon dioxide	+	Water
$CaCO_3$	+	HCl	⟶	$CaCl_2$	+	CO_2	+	H_2O

1 Balance the equation.

- There are **more** chlorine atoms and hydrogen atoms on the products side than on the reactants side, so **balance** chlorine by doubling the amount of hydrochloric acid.
- The amount of chlorine and hydrogen on both sides is now equal. This gives you a **balanced equation**.

2 Include the state symbols

$$CaCO_3(s) + 2HCl(aq) \longrightarrow CaCl_2(aq) + CO_2(g) + H_2O(l)$$

Relative Atomic Mass (A_r)

The **relative atomic mass** (A_r)...

- compares the mass of one **atom** to the mass of other atoms
- is found at the top of the symbol of each element in the periodic table.

This number is used because atoms are too small for their actual atomic mass to be of much use.

$^{65}_{30}$ **Zn** Relative atomic mass of zinc is 65.

$^{16}_{8}$ **O** Relative atomic mass of oxygen is 16.

Key Words

Atom • Biosphere • DNA • Element • Product • Reactant • Relative atomic mass

Chemicals of the Natural Environment

Extracting Useful Materials

Ores are rocks that contain varying amounts of **minerals** from which **metals** can be extracted.

Sometimes, very large amounts of ores need to be mined in order to recover a small percentage of valuable minerals, for example, copper.

The method of extraction depends on how reactive the metal is.

Metals which are less reactive than carbon (e.g. zinc, iron and copper) can be extracted from their oxides by heating with carbon:

- The metal oxide is reduced as it has lost oxygen.
- The carbon is oxidised as it has gained oxygen.

For example, zinc can be extracted from zinc oxide by heating it with carbon:

HT Calculating a Metal's Mass

If you are given its formula, you can calculate the mass of metal that can be extracted from a substance:

1. Write down the formula.
2. Work out the relative formula mass.
3. Work out the percentage mass of the metal.
4. Work out the mass of the metal.

Example

Find the mass of Zn that can be extracted from 100g of ZnO.

1. ZnO
2. Relative formula mass = 65 + 16 = 81
3. Percentage of zinc present

$$= \frac{A_r \ Zn}{M_r \ ZnO} \times 100 = \frac{65}{81} \times 100 = 80\%$$

4. In 100g of ZnO, there will be $\frac{80}{100} \times 100$

= **80g of Zn**

If you were given the equation of a reaction, you could find the ratio of the mass of the reactant to the mass of the product.

$$2ZnO(s) \ + \ C \longrightarrow \ 2Zn \ + \ CO_2$$

Relative formula mass:

> Work out the M_r of each substance

$$(2 \times 81) + 12 = (2 \times 65) + 44$$
$$162 + 12 = 130 + 44$$
$$174 = 174$$

Therefore, 162g of ZnO produces 130g of Zn.

So, 1g of ZnO $= \frac{130}{162} = 0.8$g of Zn

and 100g of Zn = 0.8 x 100 = 80g of Zn.

Chemicals of the Natural Environment

Electrolysis

Electrolysis is the breaking down of an **electrolyte** using an **electric current**.

The process is used to extract **reactive metals** from their ores because they're too reactive to be extracted by heating with carbon.

Ionic compounds conduct electricity when they are...
- molten
- dissolved in solution.

This is because their **ions** are free to move throughout the liquid.

When an ionic compound melts, electrostatic forces between the charged ions in the crystal lattice are broken down and the ions are free to move.

When a direct current is passed through a molten ionic compound...
- positively charged ions are attracted towards the **negative electrode**
- negatively charged ions are attracted towards the **positive electrode**.

For example, in the electrolysis of molten lead bromide...
- positively charged lead ions are attracted towards the **negative electrode**, forming the lead (a metal)
- negatively charged bromide ions are attracted towards the **positive electrode**, forming the bromine (a non-metal).

HT When ions get to the oppositely charged electrode they are **discharged**, i.e. they lose their charge.

For example, in the electrolysis of molten lead bromide the non-metal ion loses electrons to the positive electrode to form a bromine atom. The bromine atom then bonds with a second atom to form a bromine molecule:

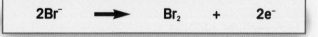

$$2Br^- \longrightarrow Br_2 + 2e^-$$

The lead ions gain electrons from the negative electrode to form a lead atom:

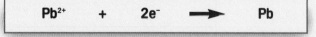

$$Pb^{2+} + 2e^- \longrightarrow Pb$$

This process completes the circuit as the electrons are exchanged at the electrodes.

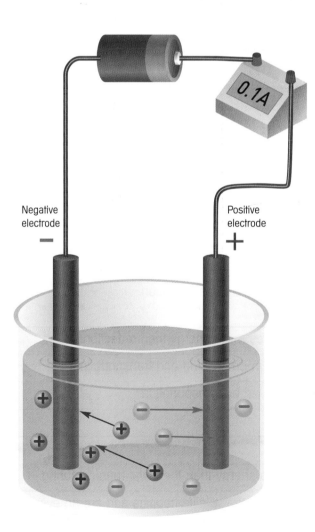

Negative electrode −

Positive electrode +

0.1A

Key Words
Compound • Current • Electrolysis • Electrolyte • Ion • Ore

Chemicals of the Natural Environment

Extracting Aluminium by Electrolysis

Aluminium is extracted from its **ore** by **electrolysis**:

1. Aluminium ore (bauxite) is purified to leave aluminium oxide.
2. Aluminium oxide is mixed with cryolite (a compound of aluminium) to lower its melting point.
3. The mixture of aluminium oxide and cryolite is melted so that the **ions** can move.
4. When a **current** passes through the molten mixture, positively charged aluminium ions move towards the **negative electrode**.
5. Aluminium is formed at the negative electrode.
6. Negatively charged oxide ions move towards the **positive electrode**.
7. Oxygen is formed at the positive electrode.

Aluminium oxide $\longrightarrow$	Aluminium	+	Oxygen
$2Al_2O_3(l) \longrightarrow$	$4Al(l)$	+	$3O_2(g)$

HT The reactions at the electrodes can be written as **half equations**. This means that you write separate equations for what is happening at each of the electrodes during electrolysis.

At the negative electrode, aluminium ions gain electrons to become neutral atoms:

$$Al^{3+}(l) \quad + \quad 3e^- \quad \xrightarrow{\text{Reduction}} \quad Al(l)$$

At the positive electrode, oxygen ions lose electrons to become neutral atoms:

$$2O^{2-}(l) \quad + \quad 4e^- \quad \xrightarrow{\text{Oxidation}} \quad O_2(g)$$

Metals and the Environment

This table shows the **environmental impacts** of extracting, using and disposing of metals.

Stage of Life Cycle	Process	Environmental Impact
Manufacture	Mining	• Lots of rock wasted. • Leaves a scar on the landscape. • Air / noise pollution.
	Processing	• Pollutants caused by transportation. • Energy usage.
	Extracting the metal	• Electrolysis uses more energy than reduction.
	Manufacturing products	• Energy usage in processing and transportation.
Use	Transport to shops / home	• Pollutants caused by transportation.
	Running product	• Energy usage.
Disposal	Reuse	• No impact.
	Recycle	• Uses a lot less energy than the initial manufacturing.
	Throw away	• Landfill sites remove wildlife habitats and are an eyesore.

Chemicals of the Natural Environment

Properties of Metals

A metal has a **giant structure** of **atoms** which is held together by a strong force of attraction called the **metallic bond**.

Metals…

- are **strong** – the ions are closely packed in a lattice structure.
- are **malleable** – they can be bent into shape or dented as the layers of metal ions can slide over each other.
- have **high melting points** – a lot of energy is needed to break the strong force of attraction between metal ions and the sea of electrons.
- **conduct electricity** – **electrons** are free to move throughout the structure. When an electrical force is applied, the electrons move along the metal in one direction.

HT In a metal crystal the positively charged metal ions are held closely together by a **'sea' of electrons**.

Lattice of positive ions →
'Sea' of electrons that are all free to move

Strong	Malleable
Closely packed lattice structure	Force applied / Force applied — Rows of ions slide over each other
High Melting Point	**Conducts Electricity**
Strong forces of attraction	Moving electrons carry the electrical charge

Uses of Metals

The properties of metals determine how they're used:

- Titanium is **strong** and is used for replacement hip joints and submarines.
- Aluminium is **malleable** and is used for drinks cans.
- Iron has a **high melting point** and is used for making saucepans.
- Copper **conducts electricity** and is used for cables and electrical switches.

Key Words

Atom • Current • Electrolysis • Electron • Ion • Ore

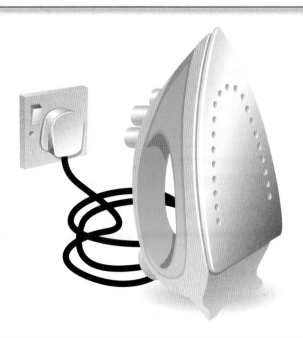

Module C5 Summary

The Earth's Resources

Atmosphere = layer of gas surrounding the Earth.

Hydrosphere = mostly made up of water and dissolved compounds.

Biosphere = made up of all the living things on Earth.

Lithosphere = rigid outer layer of the Earth, made up of the crust and mantle.

Chemical cycles – movement of chemicals between different spheres.

Chemicals of the Atmosphere

Chemicals that make up the atmosphere are **gases** at $20°$ because they have low boiling points.

Gases have weak forces of attraction between molecules so only need small amounts of energy to break forces.

HT **Covalent bonds** = strong electrostatic attraction between positive nuclei and shared pair of negative electrons.

Chemicals of the Hydrosphere

Ionic compounds – ions are electrostatically attracted to each other to form a 3-D giant crystal lattice with high melting and boiling points. **Conduct electricity** when dissolved in water.

Salts = dissolved ionic compounds.

Polar molecule = water molecule is bent because shared electrons are nearer the oxygen atom than the hydrogen atoms. So, atoms have small charges.

Water molecule attracted to crystal lattice ➡ ion breaks away ➡ ion moves freely through water.

Chemicals of the Lithosphere

The three most abundant elements in the lithosphere are…
*   oxygen
*   silicon
*   aluminium.

Silicon Dioxide

Silicon dioxide = compound made from silicon and oxygen. Found in Earth's crust. Forms **giant covalent structure**.

Silicon dioxide ➡ quartz in granite ➡ main constituent of sandstone

Properties of silicon dioxide = hard, high melting and boiling point, electrical insulator and insoluble in water.

Module C5 Summary

Chemicals of the Biosphere

Contains three groups of molecules:
- Carbohydrates.
- Proteins.
- DNA.

Carbohydrates – contain carbon, oxygen and hydrogen.

Proteins = polymers made from amino acid monomers joined together.

DNA = large, complex molecule.

Extracting Useful Materials

Ores = rocks containing varying amounts of minerals from which metals can be extracted.

Metals less reactive than carbon ➡ extracted by heating with carbon.

Metal **reduced** ➡ **lost** oxygen.

Carbon **oxidised** ➡ **gained** oxygen.

Electrolysis

Electrolysis = breaking down of an electrolyte using an electric current. Used to extract reactive metals from their ores.

Positive ions ➡ negative electrode.

Negative ions ➡ positive electrode.

(HT) When ions get to oppositely charged electrodes they are **discharged**.

Half equations = written to describe what is happening at each of the electrodes during electrolysis.

Properties of Metals

Metals…
- are strong
- are malleable
- high melting points
- conduct electricity.

(HT) Metal crystal – positively charged metal ions held closely together by 'sea' of electrons.

Module C5 Practice Questions

1 Use the words from the list below to complete the following sentences:

Earth	gas	outer	water	mantle	compounds
organisms	biosphere	crust	atmosphere	animals	lithosphere

a) The .... is the layer of .... surrounding the Earth.

b) The hydrosphere is all the .... on the Earth and contains dissolved

....

c) The .... is all the living .... on the Earth including plants,

.... and microorganisms.

d) The .... is the rigid .... layer of the ....

made of the .... and part of the .... just below it.

2 Use the flow chart of the nitrogen cycle to answer the following questions.

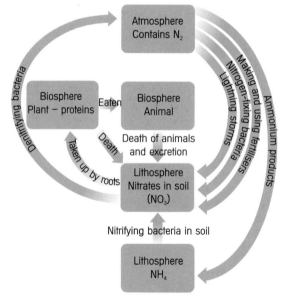

a) Which sphere does N_2 in the atmosphere move into?

....

b) What happens when plants and animals die?

....

c) How do nitrates in the soil return to the atmosphere?

....

3 a) Why is the shape of a water molecule bent?

_____

b) Why is a lot of energy needed to separate water molecules?

_____

c) How do small charges on water molecules help them dissolve ionic compounds?

_____

_____

4 Silicon dioxide forms a giant covalent structure. Which three of the following properties would you expect this compound to have? Tick the correct options.

A Strong. ◯   **B** Conducts electricity. ◯

C Insoluble in water. ◯   **D** Low melting and boiling points. ◯

5 Which three very important groups of molecules make up a large part of the biosphere?

a) _____ **b)** _____ **c)** _____

6 How does the structure of a metal explain the following:

a) Why they are malleable. _____

b) Why they conduct electricity. _____

c) Why they have high melting points. _____

7 The stages **A–G** explain how aluminium is extracted using electrolysis. Number the stages **1–7** to show the correct order.

A Aluminium is formed at the negative electrode.

B Aluminium oxide is mixed with cryolite to lower its melting point.

C When a current passes through the molten mixture, positively charged ions move towards the negative electrode.

D Negatively charged oxide ions move towards the positive electrode.

E Aluminium ore is purified to leave aluminium oxide.

F Oxygen is formed at the positive electrode.

G The mixture of aluminium oxide and cryolite is melted so that the ions can move.

◯
◯
◯
◯
◯
◯
◯

Electric Circuits

Static Electricity

When you rub two objects together they become **electrically charged** as electrons (which are negatively charged) are transferred from one object to the other:

- The object receiving the electrons becomes negatively charged.
- The object giving up electrons becomes positively charged.

The electrical charge is called static electricity.

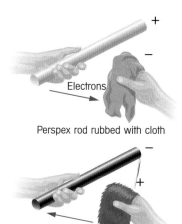

Electrons

Perspex rod rubbed with cloth

Electrons

Ebonite rod rubbed with fur

Repulsion and Attraction

When two charged materials are brought together, they exert a force on each other:

- Two materials with the same type of charge **repel** each other.
- Two materials with different charges **attract** each other.

For example, if you move...

- a positively charged Perspex rod near to another positively charged Perspex rod suspended on a string, the suspended rod will be **repelled,**
- a negatively charged ebonite rod near to a positively charged suspended Perspex rod, the suspended Perspex rod will be **attracted.**

N.B. You would get the same result with two ebonite rods.

N.B. You would get the same result if the rods were the other way round.

Electric Currents

An **electric current** is a **flow of charge**. It is measured in **amperes** (amps).

In an electric circuit...

- the components and wires are full of charges that are free to move
- the battery causes the free charges to move
- the charges are not used up but flow in a continuous loop.

In **metal conductors** there are lots of charges free to move, but in **insulators** there are no charges free to move. Metals contain **free electrons** in their structure, which move to create an **electric current**.

Key Words

Alternating current • Current • Direct current • Electron • Force • Potential difference • Static electricity • Voltage

Circuit Symbols

Standard symbols are used to represent components in circuits.

Cell	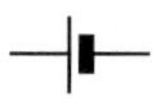	Fixed resistor	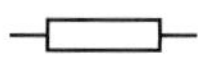
Power supply (battery)	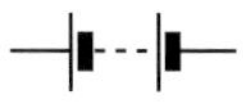	Variable resistor	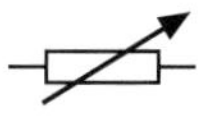
Filament lamp	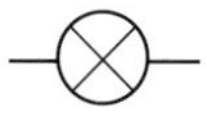	Thermistor	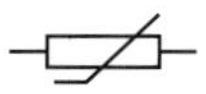
Switch (open) (closed)	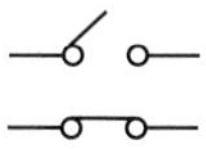	Voltmeter	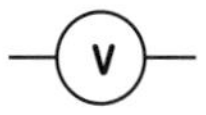
Light dependent resistor (LDR)	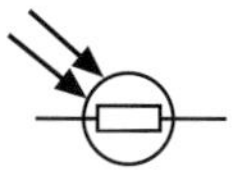	Ammeter	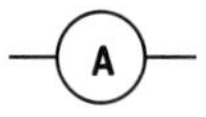

Types of Current

A **direct current** (d.c.) always flows in the same direction. Cells and batteries supply direct current.

An **alternating current** (a.c.) changes the direction of flow back and forth continuously and is used for mains electricity. The mains supply voltage to your home is 230 volts.

HT a.c. is used for mains supply instead of d.c.. This is because...
- it's easier to generate
- it can be distributed more efficiently.

Potential Difference and Current

Potential difference is another name for **voltage**:
- It's a measure of the 'push' of the battery on the charges in the circuit.
- It's measured in **volts** (V) using a **voltmeter** connected in parallel across the component.

A bulb with 3 volts across it is taking 3 joules of energy from every unit of charge. This energy is given off as heat and light.

The greater the potential difference (or voltage) across a component, the greater the current will be.

When you add more batteries in series, the voltage and the current increase.

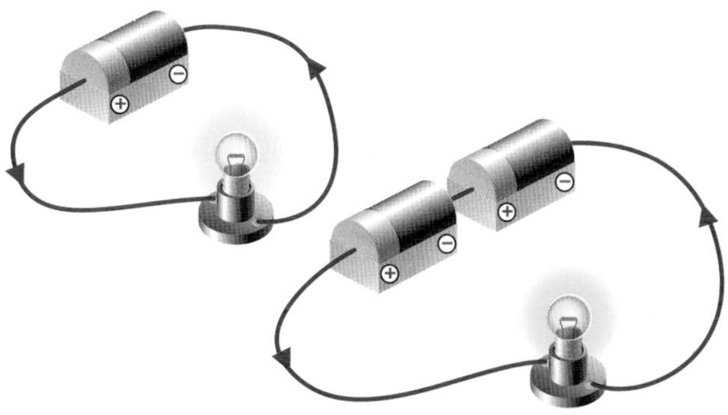

HT When you add more batteries in parallel...
- the total potential difference and current remain the same
- each battery supplies less current.

Electric Circuits

Resistance and Current

Components **resist** the flow of **charge** through them. Examples of components are…
- resistors
- lamps
- motors.

The connecting wires in the circuit have some resistance but it's so small that it's usually ignored.

The **greater the resistance** in a circuit, the **smaller the** current will be.

Two lamps together in a circuit with one cell have a certain resistance. If you include another cell in the circuit it provides…
- a greater potential difference
- a larger **current**.

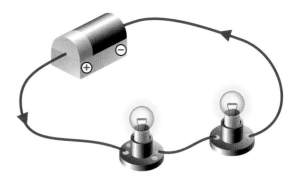

When you add resistors in **series** the battery has to push charges through more resistors so the **resistance increases**.

When you add resistors in **parallel** there are more paths for the charges to flow along so the total **resistance reduces** and the total **current increases**.

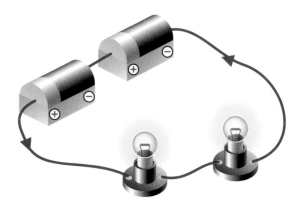

When an electric current flows through a component it causes the component to heat up. This heating effect is large enough to make a lamp filament glow.

> **HT** As the current flows…
> - moving charges collide with the stationary atoms in the wire giving them energy
> - the increase in energy causes the component to heat up.

Calculating Resistance

You can calculate resistance using this formula:

$$\text{Resistance (ohm, } \Omega) = \frac{\text{Potential difference (volt, V)}}{\text{Current (ampere, A)}}$$

where I is current

$$\frac{V}{I \times R}$$

> **HT** You can work out the voltage or current by rearranging the resistance formula.

Example

A circuit has a current of 0.2 amps and a bulb with a resistance of 15 ohms. What is the reading on the voltmeter?

Potential difference = Current x Resistance
= 0.2A x 15Ω
= **3V**

Example

A circuit has a current of 3 amps and a potential difference of 6V. What is the resistance?

$$\text{Resistance} = \frac{\text{Potential difference}}{\text{Current}} = \frac{6V}{3A} = 2\Omega$$

Current–Potential Difference Graphs

As long as a component's resistance stays constant, the current through the resistor is **directly proportional** to the voltage across the resistor. This is regardless of which direction the current is flowing.

This means that a graph showing current through the component, and voltage across the component, will be a **straight line** through 0.

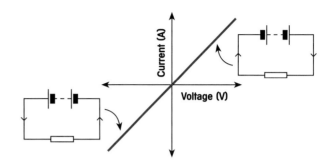

Thermistors and LDRs

The resistance of a **thermistor** depends on its temperature. As the temperature increases…
- its resistance decreases
- more current flows.

The resistance of a **light dependent resistor (LDR)** depends on light intensity. As the amount of light falling on it increases…
- its resistance decreases
- more current flows.

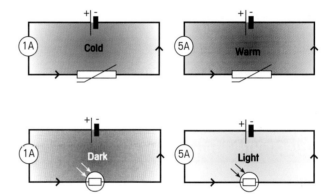

Series Circuits

In series circuits…
- the current flowing through each component is the same, i.e. $A_1 = A_2 = A_3$
- the potential difference across the components adds up to the potential difference across the battery, i.e. $V_1 = V_2 + V_3$
- the potential difference is largest across components with the greatest resistance.

HT The total energy, transferred to each unit charge by the battery, must equal the total amount of energy transferred from the charge by the component.

More energy is transferred from the charge flowing through a greater resistance because it takes more energy to push the current through the resistor.

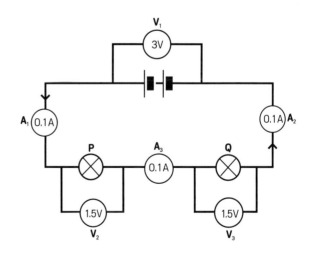

Key Words

Current • Potential difference • Resistance • Voltage

Electric Circuits

Parallel Circuits

In parallel circuits with one component per parallel path...

- the **current** flowing through each component depends on the **resistance** of each component
- the total current running from (and back to) the battery is equal to the sum of the current through each of the parallel components, i.e. $A_1 = A_2 + A_3 = A_4$
- the current is smallest through the component with the greatest resistance.

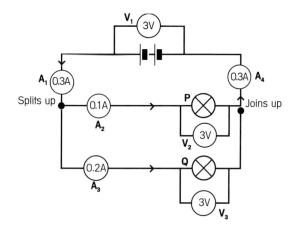

(HT) The current through each component is the same as if it were the only component present. If a second identical component is added in parallel...

- the same current flows through each component
- the total current through the battery increases.

The same **voltage** causes more current to flow through a smaller resistance than a bigger one.

The **potential difference** across each component is equal to the potential difference of the battery.

Electromagnetic Induction

When you move a magnet into a coil of wire, a **voltage** is induced between the ends of the wire because the magnetic field is being cut.

If the ends of the coil are connected to make a complete circuit, a **current** will be induced.

This is called **electromagnetic induction**.

Moving the magnet into the coil induces a current in one direction. You can then induce a current in the opposite direction by...

- moving the magnet out of the coil
- moving the other pole of the magnet into the coil.

If there's no movement of the coil or magnet, there's no induced current.

Moving the Magnet into the Coil

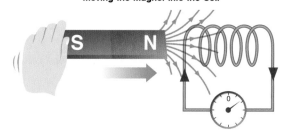

Moving the Magnet out of the Coil

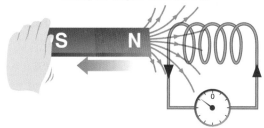

Moving the Other Pole of the Magnet into the Coil

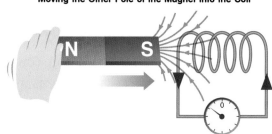

Key Words

Current • Resistance • Voltage

The Electric Generator

Mains electricity is produced by **generators**. Generators use the principle of **electromagnetic induction** to generate electricity by rotating a magnet inside a coil.

The size of the induced voltage can be increased by...
- increasing the speed of rotation of the magnet
- increasing the strength of the magnetic field
- increasing the number of turns on the coil
- placing an iron core inside the coil.

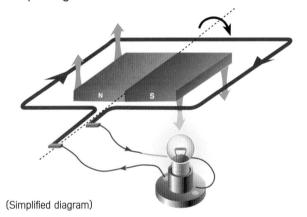

(Simplified diagram)

(HT) As the magnet rotates, the **voltage** induced in the coil changes direction and size as shown in the diagram.

The **current** that's produced is an **alternating current** as it reverses its direction of flow every half turn of the magnet.

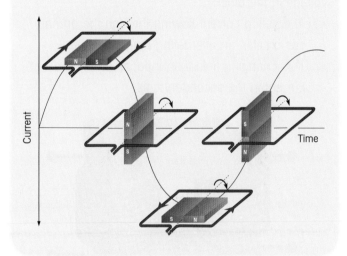

Power

When charge flows through a component, **energy is transferred** to the component.

Power is a measure of the rate of energy transfer and is measured in watts (W).

You can calculate power using the following formula:

Power (watt, W)	=	Potential difference (volt, V)	X	Current (ampere, A)	$\dfrac{P}{V \times I}$

where I is the current

Example

An electric motor works at a current of 3A and a potential difference of 24V. What is the power of the motor?

Power = Potential Difference x Current
= 24V x 3A
= **72W**

(HT) You can work out the potential difference or current by rearranging the power formula.

Example

A 4W light bulb works at a current of 2A. What is the potential difference?

$$\text{Potential difference} = \frac{\text{Power}}{\text{Current}} = \frac{4W}{2A} = 2V$$

Electric Circuits

Transformers

Transformers are used to change the **voltage** of an **alternating current**. They consist of two coils of wire, called the primary and secondary coils, wrapped around a soft iron core.

When two coils of wire are close to each other, a changing magnetic field in one coil can induce a voltage in the other:

- Alternating current flowing through the primary coil creates an alternating magnetic field.
- This changing field then induces an alternating current in the secondary coil.

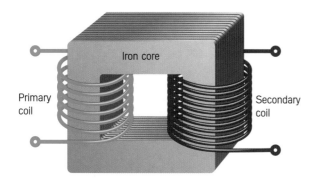

Iron core

Primary coil

Secondary coil

HT The amount by which a transformer changes the voltage depends on the number of turns on the primary and secondary coils. You need to be able to use this equation:

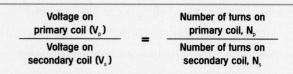

Voltage on primary coil (V_p) / Voltage on secondary coil (V_s)	=	Number of turns on primary coil, N_p / Number of turns on secondary coil, N_s

Example

A transformer has 1000 turns on the primary coil and 200 turns on the secondary coil. If a voltage of 250V is applied to the primary coil, what is the voltage across the secondary coil?

$$\frac{250}{V_s} = \frac{1000}{200}$$

$$250 = 5V_s$$

$$V_s = \frac{250}{5}$$

$$V_s = \textbf{50V}$$

Energy

Energy is measured is **joules**. A joule is a very small amount of energy so a domestic electricity meter measures the energy transfer in **kilowatt hours**.

You can calculate energy transfer in joules and kilowatt hours using the following formula:

Energy transferred (joule, J) (kilowatt hour, kWh)	=	Power (watt, W) (Kilowatt, kW)	X	Time (second, s) (hour, h)

Example 1

A 30W light bulb is switched on for 45 seconds. What is the energy transferred in joules?

Energy transferred = Power x Time
= 30W x 45s
= **1350J**

Example 2

A 2000W electric hot plate is switched on for 90 minutes. What is the energy transferred in kWh?

Energy transferred = 2kW x 1.5h
= **3kWh**

HT You can work out the power or time by rearranging the energy transfer formula.

Example

A hairdryer is switched on for 6 minutes and the total energy transferred is 0.2kWh. What is the power rating of the hairdryer?

Power = $\dfrac{\text{Energy transferred}}{\text{Time}}$ = $\dfrac{0.2\text{kWh}}{0.1\text{h}}$ = **2kW**

Cost of Electricity

If you know the power, time and cost per kilowatt hour, you can calculate the cost of the electrical energy used. The formula is as follows:

Total cost	=	Number of units (kWh)	X	Cost per unit

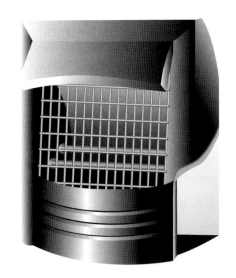

Example

A 2000W electric fire is switched on for 30 minutes. How much does it cost if electricity is 8p per unit (kWh)?

Energy transferred = 2kW x 0.5h

= 1kWh (or 1 unit)

Cost = 1kWh x 8p

= **8p**

Efficiency of Appliances

The greater the proportion of energy that is usefully transferred, the more **efficient** the appliance is.

You can calculate efficiency using this formula:

$$\text{Efficiency (\%)} = \frac{\text{Energy usefully transferred}}{\text{Total energy supplied}} \times 100$$

Electrical Appliance	Energy In	Useful Energy Out	Efficiency
Light bulb	100 joules/s	Light: 20 joules/s	$\frac{20}{100}$ x 100% = **20%**
Kettle	2000 joules/s	Heat (in water): 1800 joules/s	$\frac{1800}{2000}$ x 100% = **90%**
Electric motor	500 joules/s	Kinetic: 300 joules/s	$\frac{300}{500}$ x 100% = **60%**
Television	200 joules/s	Light: 20 joules/s Sound: 30 joules/s	$\frac{50}{200}$ x 100% = **25%**

Key Words

Alternating current • Efficiency • Transformer • Voltage

Module P5 Summary

Static Electricity

Static electricity is created when two objects are rubbed together.

Objects receiving electrons ➡ negatively charged.

Objects giving up electrons ➡ positively charged.

Two materials with **same** charges ➡ **repel** each other.

Two materials with **different** charges ➡ **attract** each other.

Current and Potential Difference

Current = flow of charge measured in amperes.

Direct current ➡ flows in same direction.

Alternating current ➡ constantly changes direction.

Metal conductors ➡ lots of charges free to move.

Insulators ➡ no charges free to move.

Potential difference = voltage ➡ measured in volts.

Greater **potential difference** across a component ➡ greater **current** through the component.

Adding batteries in series ➡ increases voltage and current.

(HT) Adding batteries in parallel ➡ potential difference and current stays same and each battery supplies less current.

Resistance

Components – resist flow of charge.

Electric current flows through component ➡ component heats up.

Greater **resistance** in a circuit ➡ **smaller** current.

Adding resistors in series ➡ increases total resistance.

Adding resistors in parallel ➡ reduces total resistance and increases current through the battery.

Current–potential difference graphs – current through resistor is directly proportional to voltage across resistor.

Thermistor – resistance depends on temperature

LDR – resistance depends on light intensity.

$$\text{Resistance (ohm, } \Omega) = \frac{\text{Potential difference (volt, V)}}{\text{Current (ampere, A)}}$$

Circuits

In **series circuits**...
- current flowing through each component is the same
- potential difference across components add up to that across the battery
- potential difference is **largest** across components with **greatest** resistance.

In **parallel circuits**...
- current flowing through each component depends on resistance
- current running to and from battery is equal to sum of current through each parallel component.
- current is **smallest** across components with **greatest** resistance.

Circuit symbols are used to represent components in circuits.

Electromagnetic Induction

When a magnet is moved into a coil of wire, a **voltage** is induced. If ends of coil are connected, a **current** is induced.

Current can be induced in opposite direction by...
- moving magnet out of coil
- moving other pole of magnet into coil.

Electric generators – use electromagnetic induction. Produce mains electricity.

(HT) Generators produce alternating current as the direction of flow is reversed every half turn of the magnet.

Transformers – used to change the voltage of an alternating current.

Power and Energy

Power = measure of the rate of energy transfer.

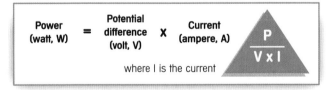

Power (watt, W)	=	Potential difference (volt, V)	X	Current (ampere, A)

where I is the current

$\dfrac{P}{V \times I}$

Energy – measured in joules. Domestic energy is measured in kilowatt hours as joules are very small amounts of energy.

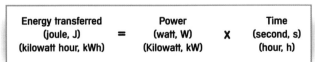

Energy transferred (joule, J) (kilowatt hour, kWh)	=	Power (watt, W) (Kilowatt, kW)	X	Time (second, s) (hour, h)

Efficiency = the proportion of energy that is usefully transferred by an appliance.

$$\text{Efficiency (\%)} = \frac{\text{Energy usefully transferred}}{\text{Total energy supplied}} \times 100$$

Module P5 Practice Questions

1 Peter has suspended a positively charged Perspex rod on a string.

   a) What will happen if Peter moves another positively charged Perspex rod near to it? ....

   b) What will happen if he moves a negatively charged ebonite rod near to it? ....

2 Draw the symbol for a cell.

3 This question is about currents.

   a) Fill in the missing words to complete the sentences below.

.... currents always flow in the same direction.

.... currents change the direction of flow back and forth continuously.

   HT **b)** Give two reasons why an alternating current is used for mains electricity.

     i) ....   **ii)** ....

4 **a)** What is another name for potential difference? ....

   b) Circle the correct option in the following sentence:

The greater the potential difference, the **lower** / **greater** the current will be.

5 **a)** A circuit has a current of 5 amps and a potential difference of 15 volts. Calculate the resistance.

   HT **b)** A circuit has a current of 0.6 amps and a lamp with a resistance of 20 ohms. Calculate the potential difference.

   c) Explain why, in series circuits, the potential difference is largest across components with the greatest resistance.

6 Sunita is experimenting with a magnet and a coil of wire. She moves the magnet into the coil to induce a current in one direction. Give two ways in which she can then induce a current in the opposite direction.

a) .... **b)** ....

7 **a)** What are transformers used for?

....

b) Briefly explain how transformers work.

....

....

HT **c)** A transformer has 2000 turns on the primary coil and 100 turns on the secondary coil. If a voltage of 400V is applied to the primary coil, what is the voltage across the secondary coil?

....

8 This question is about energy.

a) What unit is energy measured in? ....

b) Why does a domestic electricity meter measure energy transfer in kilowatt hours?

....

c) A 40W light bulb is switched on for 30 seconds. Calculate the amount of energy transferred in joules.

....

d) A 1800W hairdryer is switched on for 30 minutes. Calculate the energy transferred in kilowatt hours.

....

9 Complete the table about the efficiency of the electrical appliances.

Electrical Appliance	Energy In	Useful Energy Out	Efficiency
Iron	2000 joules/s	Heat: 1600 joules/s	**a)**
Radio	200 joules/s	Sound: 60 joules/s	**b)**
Computer	400 joules/s	Light: 180 joules/s Sound: 80 joules/s	**c)**

Brain and Mind

The Central Nervous System

A **stimulus** is a change in an organism's environment.

Animals respond to **stimuli** in order to keep themselves in suitable conditions for survival.

An animal's response is coordinated by the **central nervous system** (**CNS**). The CNS (brain and spinal cord) is connected to the body by the **peripheral nervous system**.

The peripheral nervous system consists of…
- **sensory neurons** which carry impulses from **receptors** to the CNS
- **motor neurons** which carry impulses from the CNS to **effectors**.

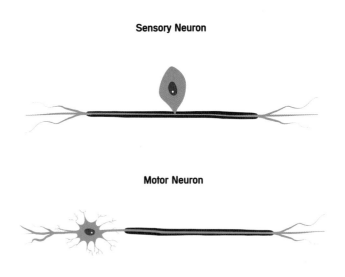

Sensory Neuron

Motor Neuron

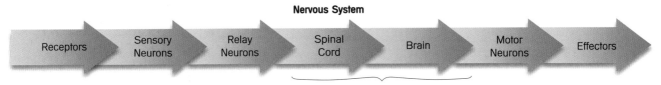

Nervous System

Receptors → Sensory Neurons → Relay Neurons → Spinal Cord → Brain → Motor Neurons → Effectors

The Central Nervous System (CNS)

Receptors and Effectors

Receptors and **effectors** can form part of complex organs, for example…
- muscle cells in a muscle
- light receptor cells in the retina of the eye
- hormone-secreting cells in a gland.

Muscle cells in a muscle – impulses travel along motor neurons and stop at the muscle cells (effectors), causing the muscle cells to contract.

Light receptors cells in the retina of the eye – the lens focuses light onto receptor cells in the retina. The receptor cells are then stimulated and send impulses along sensory neurons to the brain.

Hormone-secreting cells in a gland – an impulse travels along a motor neuron and stops at the hormone-secreting cells in glands (effectors). This triggers the release of the hormone into the bloodstream.

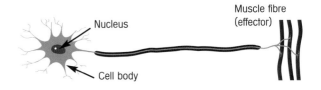

A Motor Neuron

Nucleus

Muscle fibre (effector)

Cell body

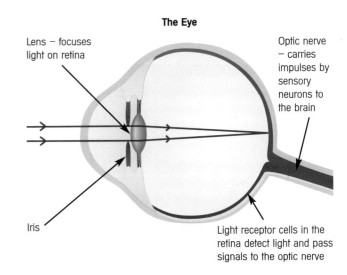

The Eye

Lens – focuses light on retina

Optic nerve – carries impulses by sensory neurons to the brain

Iris

Light receptor cells in the retina detect light and pass signals to the optic nerve

Neurons

Neurons are specially adapted cells that carry an **electrical signal** when stimulated:

- They are **elongated** (lengthened) to make connections between different parts of your body.
- They have **branched endings** so that a single neuron can act on many other neurons or effectors.

In **motor neurons** the cytoplasm forms a long fibre surrounded by a cell membrane called an **axon**.

Some axons are surrounded by a fatty sheath, which...

- insulates the neuron from neighbouring cells
- increases the speed at which the nerve impulse is transmitted.

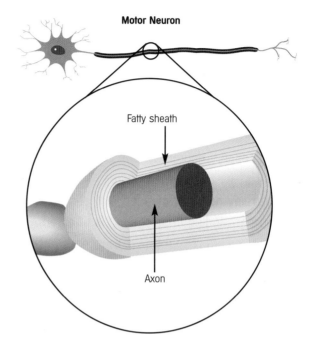

Motor Neuron

Fatty sheath

Axon

Synapses

Synapses are the gaps between adjacent neurons.

HT Impulses are transferred between neurons in the following way:

1. A nerve impulse reaches the synapse through the sensory neuron.
2. The impulse triggers the release of chemicals, called neurotransmitters, into the synapse.
3. Neurotransmitters diffuse across the synapse and bind with receptor molecules on the membrane of a motor neuron.
4. A nerve impulse is sent through the motor neuron.

The receptor molecules only bind with certain chemicals to start a nerve impulse in the motor neuron.

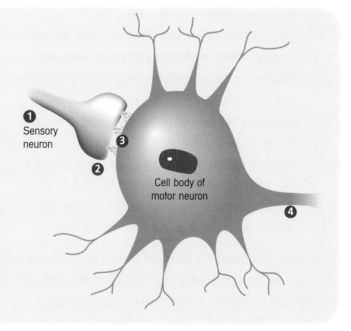

Sensory neuron

Cell body of motor neuron

Key Words

Axon • Central nervous system • Effector • Neuron • Receptor • Stimulus • Synapse

Brain and Mind

Reflex Actions

A **reflex action** is a fast, automatic, involuntary response to a **stimulus**.

The basic pathway for a reflex arc is as follows:

1. A **receptor** is stimulated (e.g. by a sharp pin).
2. This causes impulses to pass along a **sensory neuron** into the spinal cord.
3. The sensory neuron **synapses** with a relay neuron, by-passing the brain.
4. The relay neuron synapses with a motor neuron, sending impulses to the **effectors**.
5. The effectors **respond** (e.g. muscles contract).

Simple reflexes like these ensure that an animal **automatically responds** to a **stimulus** in a way that helps it to survive, for example...
- finding food
- sheltering from predators
- finding a mate.

A majority of the behaviour displayed by simple animals is the result of **reflex actions**. The disadvantage of this is that the animals have difficulty responding to new situations.

Reflex Action Pathway

Stimulus → Receptor → Sensory Neuron → Relay Neuron (in spinal cord) → Motor Neuron → Effector → Response

Simple Reflexes in Humans

Newborn babies exhibit a range of simple reflexes:
- **Stepping reflex** – when held under its arms in an upright position, with feet on a firm surface, a baby makes walking movements with legs.
- **Startle (or moro) reflex** – baby shoots out arms and legs when startled.
- **Grasping reflex** – baby tightly grasps a finger that is placed in its hand.
- **Rooting reflex** – baby turns head and opens mouth ready to feed when its cheek is stroked.
- **Sucking reflex** – baby sucks on a finger (or mother's nipple) that is put in its mouth.

Adults also display a range of simple reflexes. For example, the **pupil reflex** in your eye stops bright light from damaging your retina. Your iris controls the amount of light that enters your eye by contracting various muscle fibres:
- In dim light, your pupil size increases to let more light in.
- In bright light, your pupil size decreases to reduce the amount of light let in.

Eye in Dim Light

Increased pupil size

Radial muscles contract

Circular muscles relax

Eye in Bright Light

Decreased pupil size

Radial muscles relax

Circular muscles contract

The Pupil Reflex

Light on retina → Impulse via optic nerve to the brain → Impulse via motor nerve to iris muscles → Pupil changes size

HT Conditioned Reflexes

A reflex response to a new stimulus can be learned by building an association between the stimulus that naturally triggers the response (**primary stimulus**) and the new stimulus (**secondary stimulus**).

The resulting reflex is called a **conditioned reflex action**.

This effect was discovered at the beginning of the 20th century by a Russian scientist named Pavlov.

Pavlov carried out the following dog experiment:

1. A bell was rung repeatedly whenever meat was shown and given to the dog.
2. Eventually, ringing the bell, without any meat present, caused the dog to salivate.

In a conditioned reflex the final response has **no direct connection** to the stimulus.

Some conditioned reflexes can increase a species' chance of survival.

For example, the caterpillar of the cinnabar moth is black and orange in colour, to warn predators that it's poisonous. After eating a few cinnabar caterpillars, a bird will start to associate these colours with a very unpleasant taste and avoid eating anything that is black and orange in colour.

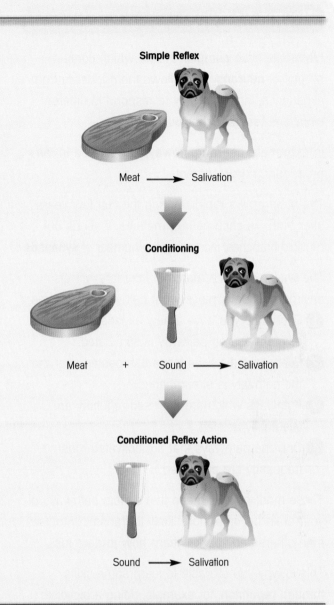

Modifying Reflex Actions

In some situations your brain can override or modify a reflex action by sending a signal, via a neuron, to the motor neuron in the reflex arc.

For example, this modification allows you to keep hold of a hot plate even though your body's natural reflex response is to drop it.

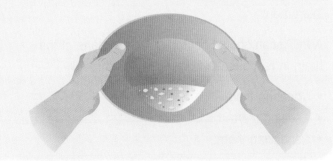

Key Words

Effector • Neuron • Receptor • Reflex action • Stimulus • Synapse

Brain and Mind

Neuron Pathways

Mammals have **complex brains** which contain billions of **neurons**. This allows them to learn from experience, including how to respond to different situations (**social behaviour**).

In mammals, **neuron pathways** are formed in the brain during development.

The brain grows rapidly during the first few years after birth. As each neuron matures, it sends out multiple branches, increasing the number of **synapses**.

The way in which a mammal interacts with its environment determines what pathways are formed:

1 Each time you have a new experience, a different neuron pathway is stimulated.

2 Every time the experience is repeated after that, the pathway is strengthened.

3 Pathways which are not used regularly are eventually deleted.

4 Only the pathways that are activated most frequently are preserved.

These modifications mean that certain pathways of your brain become more likely to transmit impulses than others and you will learn how to do a task.

This is why you are able to learn some skills through **repetition**, for example, riding a bicycle, revising for an exam or playing a musical instrument.

A **PET scan** shows neuron activity in parts of the brain in response to learning words through…

- hearing them
- seeing them
- speaking them.

The areas which are stimulated the most, develop more synapses between neurons.

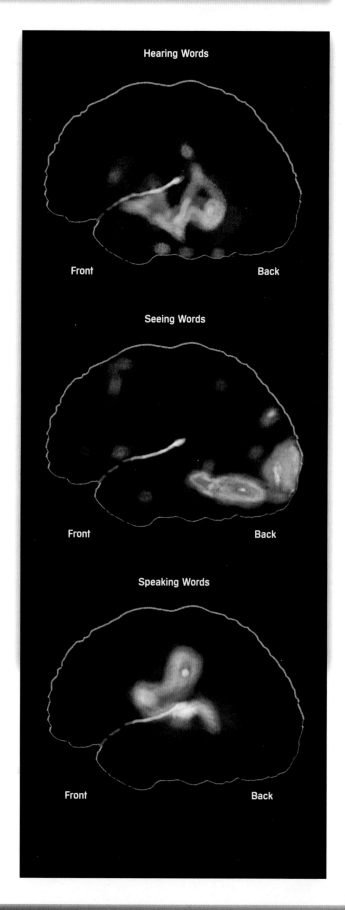

Hearing Words

Front   Back

Seeing Words

Front   Back

Speaking Words

Front   Back

Feral Children

Evidence suggests that children only learn some skills at particular stages in their development.

One example of evidence showing this comes from the study of language development in 'feral children'.

Feral children have been isolated from society in some way, so they don't go through the normal development process.

This isolation can be deliberate (e.g. keeping a child alone in a locked room) or accidental (e.g. through being shipwrecked).

In the absence of any other humans, the children don't ever gain the ability to talk other than to make rudimentary grunting noises.

Learning a language later in development is a much harder and slower process.

Child Development

After children are born there are a series of developmental milestones which can be checked to see if development is following normal patterns.

If the milestones are missing or late it could mean that…
- there are neurological problems
- the child is lacking stimulation.

For example…
- at three months, babies should be able to lift their heads when held to someone's shoulder
- at 12 months, babies should be able to hold a cup and drink from it.

Adapting

The variety of potential pathways in the brain makes it possible for animals to **adapt** to new situations.

For example…
- dogs can be trained to follow spoken commands
- dolphins in captivity can be trained to collect food from a person's hand.

Key Words

Neuron • Synapse

Brain and Mind

Coordination of Senses

The **cerebral cortex** is the part of your brain most concerned with...

- intelligence
- memory
- language
- consciousness.

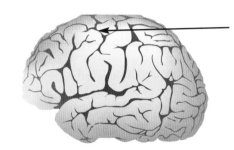

Cerebral cortex

Mapping the Cortex

Scientists have used different methods to map the regions of the cerebral cortex:

- Physiological techniques.
- Electronic techniques.
- Magnetic Resonance Images (MRI) scanning.

Physiological techniques – damage to different parts of the brain can produce different problems, e.g. memory loss, paralysis, or speech loss. Studying the effects of this has led to an understanding of which parts of the brain control different functions.

Electronic techniques – an electroencephalogram (EEG) is a visual record of the electrical activity generated by **neurons** in the brain. Electrodes are placed on the scalp to pick up the electrical signals. By stimulating the patient's **receptors**, the parts of the brain which respond can be mapped.

Magnetic Resonance Imaging (MRI) scanning – this is a relatively new technique that can be used to produce images of different cross-sections of the brain. The computer-generated picture uses colour to represent different levels of electrical activity. The activity in the brain changes depending on what the person is doing or thinking.

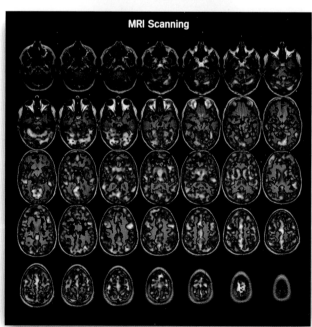

MRI Scanning

Key Words

Cerebral cortex • Neuron • Receptor • Synapse

Memory

Memory is the ability to **store** and **retrieve** information.

Scientists have produced models to try to explain how the brain does this but, so far, none have been able to provide an good enough explanation.

Verbal memory can be divided into…

* **short-term memory** – stores a limited amount of information for a limited amount of time
* **long-term memory** – stores an unlimited amount of information.

(HT) You're more likely to remember information if…
* it's repeated (especially over an extended period of time)
* there's a strong **stimulus** associated with it, for example colour, light, smell or sound
* you can see a pattern in it or impose a pattern on it, e.g. the order of the planets can be remembered by imposing a pattern: **M**y **v**ery **e**asy **m**ethod **j**ust **s**peeds **u**p **n**aming **p**lanets - **M**ercury, **V**enus, **E**arth, **M**ars, **J**upiter, **S**aturn, **U**ranus, **N**eptune and **P**luto.

Drugs and the Nervous System

Some drugs and toxins affect the nervous system by changing the speed at which nerve impulses travel to the brain.

They can also…
* send false signals to the brain
* prevent nerve impulses from travelling across **synapses**
* overload the nervous system with too many nerve impulses.

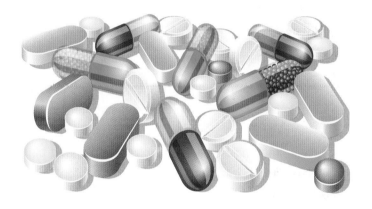

(HT) **Serotonin** is a chemical transmitter used in the **central nervous system** and is associated with feeling happy.

Serotonin passes across the brain's synapses, landing on receptor molecules. Serotonin not on a receptor is absorbed back into the transmitting neuron by the transporter molecules.

Ecstasy (MDMA) blocks the transporter sites causing serotonin to build up in the synapse. This causes…
* serotonin concentrations in the brain to increase
* the user to experience feelings of elation.

The neurons are harmed in this process and memory loss can be caused in the long term.

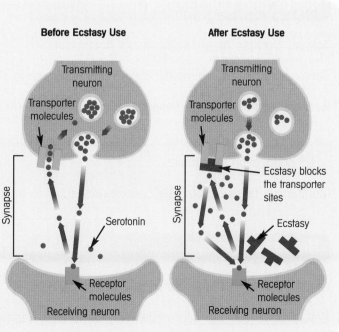

Before Ecstasy Use

Transmitting neuron

Transporter molecules

Synapse

Serotonin

Receptor molecules

Receiving neuron

After Ecstasy Use

Transmitting neuron

Transporter molecules

Synapse

Ecstasy blocks the transporter sites

Ecstasy

Receptor molecules

Receiving neuron

Module B6 Summary

The Central Nervous System

Stimulus = change in organism's environment.

Central nervous system = brain and spinal cord ➡ coordinates animal's responses.

Neurons = specially adapted cells that carry electrical signals when stimulated.

Peripheral nervous system = sensory neurons + motor neurons.

Sensory neurons ➡ carry impulses from receptors to CNS.

Motor neurons ➡ carry impulses from CNS to effectors.

Sensory Neuron

Motor Neuron

Synapses

Synapses = gaps between adjacent neurons.

(HT) Impulses are transferred between neurons in the following way:
1. Nerve impulse moves through sensory neuron.
2. Chemical neurotransmitters are released into synapse.
3. Neurotransmitters diffuse across synapse and bind with receptors on motor neuron.
4. Nerve impulse is sent through motor neuron.

Reflex and Conditioned Actions

Actions increase an animal's chance of survival.

Reflex action = fast, automatic, involuntary response to stimulus.

Receptor stimulated ➡ sensory neuron ➡ relay neuron ➡ motor neuron ➡ effector ➡ response.

(HT) Conditioned reflex action = association between primary and secondary stimulus. Final response has no direct connection to stimulus.

Modifying a reflex action ➡ brain sends signal to motor neuron.

Neuron Pathways

Neuron pathways form in brain during development.

New experience ➡ neuron pathway stimulated. Repeat experiences strengthens pathways. So skills can be leant through repetition.

Children's Development

Feral children = children who have been isolated at crucial stages of development.

If development milestones missing / late = neurological problems or lacking stimulation.

Variety of potential pathways in brain ➡ animals can adapt to new situations.

Brain

Cerebral cortex deals with...
- intelligence
- memory
- language
- consciousness.

Physiological techniques = studies effects of damage to the brain.

Electronic techniques = visual record of electrical activity generated by neurons in brain.

MRI scans = records different levels of electrical activity of the brain.

Memory

Memory = ability to store and retrieve information.

Short-term memory ➡ limited information for limited time period.

Long-term memory ➡ unlimited amount of information.

(HT) Information is easier to remember if...
- it's repeated
- there a strong stimulus attached
- there's a pattern to it.

Drugs and the Nervous System

Drugs and toxins...
- affect the nervous system by changing the speed of nerve impulses sent to the brain
- send false signals to brain
- prevent nerve impulses from travelling across synapses
- overload nervous system.

(HT) Serotonin = chemical transmitter used in nervous system.

Ecstasy ➡ causes a build up of serotonin in brain ➡ damages neurons and can lead to memory loss.

Module B6 Practice Questions

1 Circle the correct options in the following sentences:

a) Animals respond to stimuli. These responses are coordinated by the **central nervous system** / **peripheral nervous system**.

b) The system making up the connections of sensory and motor neurons is called the **central nervous system** / **peripheral nervous system**.

c) The brain is an example of an organ in the **central nervous system** / **peripheral nervous system**.

2 What type of neurons do the diagrams below show?

a) ....

b) ....

3 What does a motor neuron do to a hormone-secreting gland when a message is sent?

....

4 Give two functions of the fatty sheath surrounding the axon.

a) ....

b) ....

5 What are synapses?

....

HT The four stages, **A**, **B**, **C** and **D**, describe the sequence of nerve impulse transmission. They are in the wrong order. Number the stages **1–4** to show the correct order. The first one has been done for you.

A Nerve impulse is sent through motor neuron. ⬡

B Chemical neurotransmitters are released into synapse. ⬡

C Neurotransmitters bind with receptors on motor neuron. ⬡

D Nerve impulse moves through sensory neuron. ①

7 Draw lines between the boxes to match the simple reflexes found in newborn babies to their descriptions.

Stepping reflex	Baby shoots out arms and legs when startled.
Startle (Moro) reflex	Baby sucks on a finger that is put into its mouth.
Grasping reflex	Baby turns head and opens mouth when its cheek is stroked.
Rooting reflex	Baby makes walking movements with legs when held under arms in an upright position.
Sucking reflex	Baby tightly grasps a finger that is placed in its hand.

HT **8** Which of these statements is an example of a conditioned reflex action? Tick the correct option.

A A man choking on a piece of sandwich. ⬭

B A girl blinking as she walks from a darkened room into daylight. ⬭

C A rabbit stinging itself on a stinging nettle and avoiding the nettles in future. ⬭

D A doctor stroking the sole of a patient's feet with a stick. ⬭

9 In the past the only way to study the brain was to analyse people who had damaged parts of their brain in accidents. Give the names of two other techniques that enable scientists to 'see' what is going on in the brain.

a) .... **b)** ....

HT **10** What is the term given to children who, either by being deliberately kept from human contact or through being stranded in the absence of humans, grow up without the ability to talk?

....

11 How do drugs in general affect the nervous system?

....

HT **12** Which drug blocks the sites in the brain's synapses where serotonin is removed?

....

Chemical Synthesis

Chemicals

Chemical synthesis is the process by which raw materials are made into useful products including…
- food additives
- fertilizers
- dyestuffs
- pigments
- pharmaceuticals
- paints.

The chemical industry makes **bulk chemicals** on a very large scale and **fine chemicals** on a much smaller scale.

The range of chemicals made in industry and laboratories in the UK is illustrated in this pie chart:

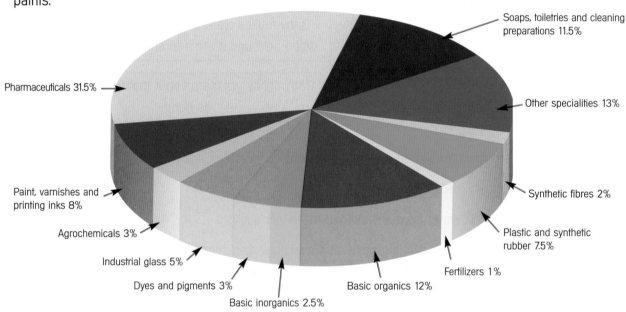

Soaps, toiletries and cleaning preparations 11.5%

Other specialities 13%

Synthetic fibres 2%

Plastic and synthetic rubber 7.5%

Fertilizers 1%

Basic organics 12%

Basic inorganics 2.5%

Dyes and pigments 3%

Industrial glass 5%

Agrochemicals 3%

Paint, varnishes and printing inks 8%

Pharmaceuticals 31.5%

Hazards

Many chemicals are **hazardous**, so it's important that you can…
- recognise the main hazard symbols
- understand the safety precautions to use.

Some examples of safety precautions are…
- wearing gloves and eye protection
- using safety screens
- not eating or drinking when working with chemicals
- not working near naked flames.

Key Words
Acid • Alkali • Compound • Ion

Corrosive

Flammable

Harmful

Irritant

Oxidising

Toxic

The pH Scale

The **pH scale** is a measure of the acidity or alkalinity of an **aqueous solution** across a 14-point scale:

- **Acids** are substances that have a pH less than 7.
- Bases are the oxides and hydroxides of metals.

Soluble bases are called **alkalis** and have a pH greater than 7.

You can measure the pH of a substance using an **indicator**, for example, universal indicator solution or a **pH meter**.

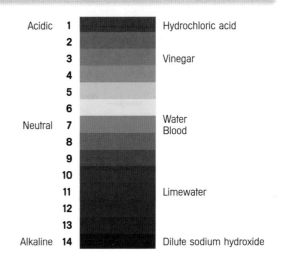

Acidic	1	Hydrochloric acid
	2	
	3	Vinegar
	4	
	5	
	6	
Neutral	7	Water / Blood
	8	
	9	
	10	
	11	Limewater
	12	
	13	
Alkaline	14	Dilute sodium hydroxide

Acidic Compounds

Acidic compounds produce aqueous **hydrogen ions**, $H^+(aq)$, when they dissolve in water.

Common Acids	Formulae to Remember	State at Room Temp.
Citric acid	–	Solid
Tartaric acid	–	Solid
Nitric acid	HNO_3	Liquid
Sulfuric acid	H_2SO_4	Liquid
Ethanoic acid	–	Liquid
Hydrogen chloride (hydrochloric acid)	HCl	Gas

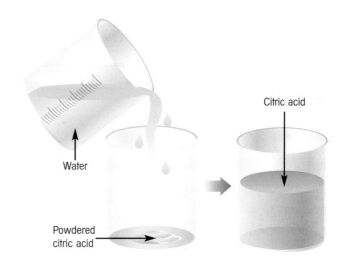

Water

Citric acid

Powdered citric acid

Alkali Compounds

Alkali compounds produce aqueous **hydroxide ions**, $OH^-(aq)$, when they dissolve in water.

Common Alkalis	Formulae to Remember
Sodium hydroxide	NaOH
Potassium hydroxide	KOH
Magnesium hydroxide	$Mg(OH)_2$
Calcium hydroxide	$Ca(OH)_2$

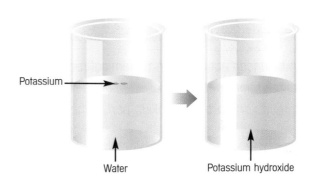

Potassium

Water

Potassium hydroxide

Chemical Synthesis

Neutralisation

When you mix together an **acid** and an **alkali** in the correct amounts they 'cancel out' each other.

Acid	+	Base	→	Neutral salt solution	+	Water

This type of reaction is called **neutralisation** because the solution that remains has a neutral pH of 7.

The **hydrogen ions** from the **acid** react with the **hydroxide ions** from the **alkali** to make water:

$$\text{H}^+(aq) \; + \; \text{OH}^-(aq) \longrightarrow \text{H}_2\text{O}(l)$$

For example, hydrochloric acid and potassium hydroxide can be neutralised:

Hydrochloric acid	+	Potassium hydroxide	→	Potassium chloride	+	Water

$$\text{HCl}(aq) \; + \; \text{KOH}(aq) \longrightarrow \text{KCl}(aq) \; + \; \text{H}_2\text{O}(l)$$

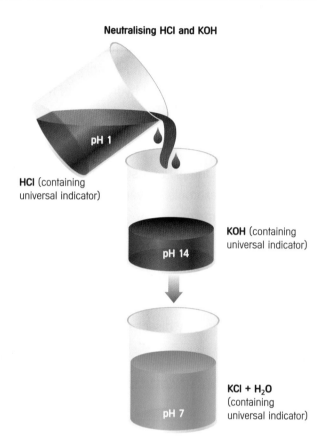

Neutralising HCl and KOH

pH 1

HCl (containing universal indicator)

KOH (containing universal indicator)

pH 14

KCl + H₂O (containing universal indicator)

pH 7

Making Salts

Acids react with metal hydroxides, metal oxides and metal carbonates to form a salt and water. When an acid reacts with a metal carbonate it also produces carbon dioxide.

Acids react with metals to form a salt and hydrogen.

The type of salt produced depends on the acid used:

- Hydro**chlor**ic acid produces **chloride** salts.
- **Sulf**uric acid produces **sulfate** salts.
- **Nitr**ic acid produces **nitrate** salts.

You need to know, and be able to write balanced equations for, the reactions of acids that produce salts.

N.B. A balanced equation for a chemical reaction shows the relative numbers of atoms and molecules of reactants and products taking part in the reaction.

(HT) You should already know how to balance unbalanced equations (see page 21).

Hydrochloric acid	+	Sodium hydroxide	→	Sodium chloride	+	Water

$$\text{HCl}(aq) \; + \; \text{NaOH}(aq) \longrightarrow \text{NaCl}(aq) \; + \; \text{H}_2\text{O}(l)$$

Hydrochloric acid	+	Copper oxide	→	Copper chloride	+	Water

$$\text{HCl}(aq) \; + \; \text{CuO}(s) \longrightarrow \text{CuCl}_2(aq) \; + \; \text{H}_2\text{O}(l)$$

Hydrochloric acid	+	Calcium carbonate	→	Calcium chloride	+	Water	+	Carbon dioxide

$$\text{HCl}(aq) \; + \; \text{CaCO}_3(s) \longrightarrow \text{CaCl}_2(aq) \; + \; \text{H}_2\text{O}(l) \; + \; \text{CO}_2(g)$$

Hydrochloric acid	+	Magnesium	→	Magnesium chloride	+	Hydrogen

$$2\text{HCl}(aq) \; + \; \text{Mg}(s) \longrightarrow \text{MgCl}_2(aq) \; + \; \text{H}_2(g)$$

Formulae of Salts

You need to remember the formulae of the salts listed in this table:

Group	Salt	Formula
Group 1	Sodium chloride	$NaCl$
Group 1	Potassium chloride	KCl
Group 1	Sodium carbonate	Na_2CO_3
Group 2	Magnesium sulfate	$MgSO_4$
Group 2	Magnesium carbonate	$MgCO_3$
Group 2	Magnesium oxide	MgO
Group 2	Calcium carbonate	$CaCO_3$
Group 2	Calcium chloride	$CaCl_2$

HT You should already know how to write formulae for **ionic compounds**. Given the formula of the salts listed in the table, you need to be able to work out the charge on each ion in a compound.

Magnesium Sulfate

Formulae of Common Gases

The formulae of the common gases are as follows:
- Chlorine, Cl_2
- Hydrogen, H_2
- Nitrogen, N_2
- Oxygen, O_2

Oxygen (O_2)

Diatomic molecule

Covalent bond

Percentage Yield

When chemical synthesis takes place, the starting materials (**reactants**) react to produce new substances (**products**). The greater the amount of reactants used, the greater the amount of product formed.

You can calculate the **percentage yield** by comparing...
- the actual yield – actual amount of product made
- the theoretical yield – amount of product you would expect to get if the reaction goes to completion.

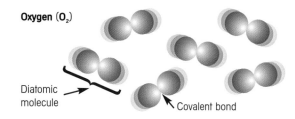

$$\text{Percentage yield} = \frac{\text{Actual yield}}{\text{Theoretical yield}} \times 100$$

Key Words

Acid • Alkali • Atom • Ion • Neutralisation • Product • Reactant • Yield

Chemical Synthesis

Chemical Synthesis

There are a number of different stages in any chemical synthesis of an inorganic **compound**:

1. Establish the **reaction** or series of reactions that are needed to make the **product**.
2. Carry out a risk assessment.
3. Carry out the reaction under suitable conditions, e.g. temperature, concentration and use of a **catalyst**.
4. Separate the product from the reaction mixture using **filtration**.
5. **Purify** the product to ensure it's not contaminated by other **products** or **reactants**:
   - Remove the water by gently heating the solution.
   - It will **evaporate** slowly to form **crystals** that will cling to the end of a cold glass rod.
   - Leave the crystals to cool.
   - Filter to separate the crystals from any solution left behind.
6. Wash the crystals with distilled water and dry in a desiccator or oven.
7. Weigh the mass and calculate the **percentage** **yield**.
8. Check the **purity** by measuring the melting point.

N.B. The purity of a product is important as impurities can kill.

Filtration

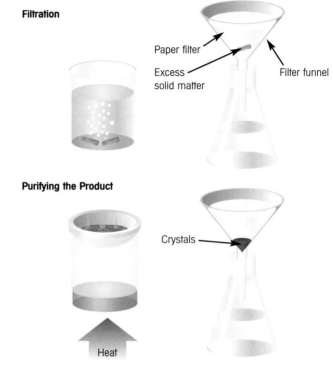

Purifying the Product

Washing the Crystals and Weighing the Mass

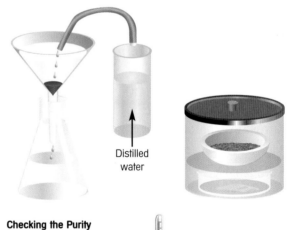

Checking the Purity

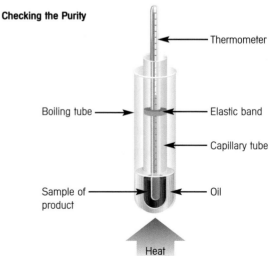

Key Words

Atom • Catalyst • Compound • Element • Product • Reactant • Relative atomic mass • Relative formula mass • Yield

Relative Atomic Mass, (A_r)

The **relative atomic mass** (A_r) of an **element** shows the mass of one **atom** in comparison to the mass of other atoms.

You can obtain the relative atomic mass of an element by looking at the periodic table.

Examples are...

- A_r of Mg = 24
- A_r of Cu = 63.5
- A_r of C = 12
- A_r of K = 39.

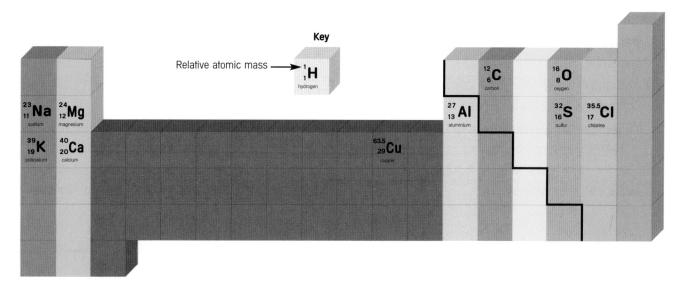

Relative Formula Mass, (M_r)

The **relative formula mass** (M_r) of a compound is the relative atomic masses of all its elements added together.

To calculate M_r you need to know...
- the formula of the compound
- the A_r of each of the atoms involved.

Example

Calculate the M_r of water, H_2O.

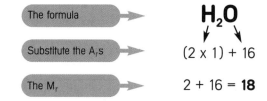

The formula	H_2O
Substitute the A_rs	(2 x 1) + 16
The M_r	2 + 16 = **18**

HT Quantity of Reactants

In chemical synthesis you need to work out how much of each reactant is required to make a known amount of product. To do this you need to know...
- how to calculate its relative atomic mass
- how to calculate its relative formula mass

- that a balanced equation shows the number of atoms or molecules of the reactants and products taking part in the reaction
- how to work out the ratio of the mass of reactants to the mass of products
- how to apply the ratio to the question.

Chemical Synthesis

HT Mass of Reactants

Example

Calculate how much calcium oxide can be produced from 50kg of calcium carbonate. (Relative atomic masses: Ca = 40, C = 12, O = 16).

1 Write down the equation.

2 Work out the M_r of each substance.

3 Check that the total mass of reactants equals the total mass of the products. If they are not the same, check your work.

4 The question only mentions calcium oxide and calcium carbonate, so you can now ignore the carbon dioxide. You just need the ratio of mass of reactant to mass of product.

5 Use the ratio to calculate how much calcium oxide can be produced.

1
$$CaCO_3 \rightarrow CaO + CO_2$$

2
$$40 + 12 + (3 \times 16) \rightarrow (40 + 16) + [12 + (2 \times 16)]$$

3
$$100 \rightarrow 56 + 44 \checkmark$$

4
$$100 : 56$$

5

If 100kg of $CaCO_3$ produces 56kg of CaO, then 1kg of $CaCO_3$ produces $\frac{56}{100}$ kg of CaO, and 50kg of $CaCO_3$ produces $\frac{56}{100} \times 50$
= **28kg of CaO**.

Mass of Products

Example

Calculate how much aluminium oxide is needed to produce 540 tonnes of aluminium. (Relative atomic masses: Al = 27, O = 16).

1 Write down the equation.

2 Work out the M_r of each substance.

3 Check that the total mass of reactants equals the total mass of the products. If they are not the same, check your work.

4 The question only mentions aluminium oxide and aluminium, so you can now ignore the oxygen. You just need the ratio of mass of reactant to mass of product.

5 Use the ratio to calculate how much aluminium oxide is needed.

1
$$2Al_2O_3 \rightarrow 4Al + 3O_2$$

2
$$2[(2 \times 27) + (3 \times 16)] \rightarrow (4 \times 27) + [3 \times (2 \times 16)]$$

3
$$204 \rightarrow 108 + 96 \checkmark$$

4
$$204 : 108$$

5

If 204 tonnes of Al_2O_3 produces 108 tonnes of Al, then $\frac{204}{108}$ tonnes is needed to produce 1 tonne of Al, and $\frac{204}{108} \times 540$ tonnes is needed to produce 540 tonnes of Al
= **1020 tonnes of Al_2O_3**.

Titration

Titration can be used to calculate the concentration of an **acid** by finding out how much **alkali** is needed to **neutralise** it.

Use this method:

1. Fill a burette with an alkali (of known concentration) and take an initial reading of the volume.
2. Accurately weigh out a sample of solid acid and dissolve it in distilled water.
3. Use a pipette to measure the aqueous acid into a conical flask. By using a pipette you will always know the amount of acid used.
4. Now, add a few drops of the indicator, phenolphthalein (it should stay colourless).
5. Add alkali from the burette to the acid in the flask drop by drop.
6. Swirl the flask to mix it well. Near the end of the reaction, the indicator will start to turn pink. When it's completely pink, it means that the acid has been neutralised.
7. Record the volume of alkali added by subtracting the amount in the burette at the end from the starting value.

N.B. You need to repeat the whole procedure until you get two results that are the same.

Alkali

Acid + phenolphthalein

White tile to see colour change.

Alkali Solution

Acid Solution

Key Words

Acid • Alkali • Neutralisation • Titration

Chemical Synthesis

Interpreting Titration Results

Example

Calculate the purity of citric acid used when…

- concentration of sodium hydroxide (NaOH) = $40g/dm^3$
- volume of sodium hydroxide = $8cm^3$
- mass of citric acid = 4g
- volume of citric acid solution = $25cm^3$

First, using the formula below, calculate the concentration of citric acid by substituting the values.

> Concentration of acid = 3 x $\dfrac{\text{Volume x Conc. NaOH}}{\text{Volume citric acid}}$

1 molecule of citric acid reacts with 3 molecules of sodium hydroxide

You must work in dm^3 when doing the calculations.
To convert cm^3 to dm^3, divide by 1000.

$$= 3 \times \frac{\left(\dfrac{8}{1000} \times 40\right)}{\left(\dfrac{25}{1000}\right)}$$

$$= \mathbf{38.4g/dm^3}$$

Then, work out the actual mass of citric acid in the sample:

> Mass = Concentration x Volume

$$= 38.4g/dm^3 \times \left(\frac{25cm^3}{1000}\right)$$

$$= \mathbf{0.96g}$$

If the mass of citric acid dissolved in $25cm^3$ is 0.96g, the mass of citric acid dissolved in $100cm^3$ of water will be 4 x 0.96 = 3.84g

> % of purity = $\dfrac{\text{Calculated mass}}{\text{Mass weighed out at start}}$ x 100

$$= \frac{3.84}{4.0} \times 100$$

$$= \mathbf{96\%}$$

Rates of Reactions

The rate of a **chemical reaction** is the amount of reaction that takes place in a given unit of time.

The rate of a chemical reaction can be found in three different ways:

1. Weighing the reaction mixture.
2. Measuring the volume of gas produced.
3. Observing the formation of a precipitate.

Weighing the reaction mixture – If one of the products is a gas, you could weigh the reaction mixture at timed intervals. The mass of the mixture will decrease as the gas is produced.

Measuring the volume of gas produced – You could use a gas syringe to measure the total volume of gas produced at timed intervals.

Observing the formation of a precipitate – This can be done by…

- watching a cross on a tile underneath the jar to see when it's no longer visible
- monitoring a colour change using a light sensor.

Weighing the Reaction Mixture

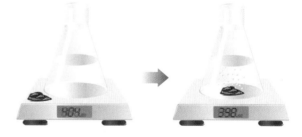

Measuring the Volume of Gas Produced

Observing the Formation of a Precipitate

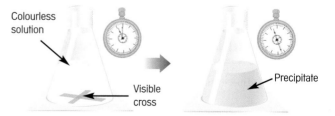

Colourless solution

Visible cross

Precipitate

Changing the Rate of Reaction

There are four important factors which affect the rate of reaction:

1. **Temperature**.
2. **Concentration**.
3. **Surface area**.
4. Use of a **catalyst**.

Temperature of the Reactants

In a **cold reaction mixture**, the particles move quite slowly which means...

- the particles will collide less often and with less energy
- fewer collisions will be successful.

In a **hot reaction mixture**, the particles move more quickly which means...

- the particles will collide more often and with greater energy
- more collisions will be successful.

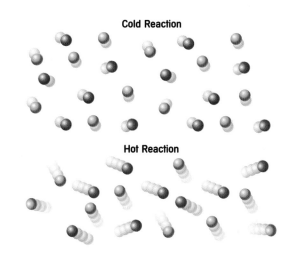

Cold Reaction

Hot Reaction

Concentration of Dissolved Reactants

In a **low concentration** reaction, there are less particles of **reactant** and the particles are spread out, which means...

- the particles will collide less often
- fewer collisions will be successful.

In a **high concentration** reaction, there are more particles of reactant and the particles are crowded close together, which means...

- the particles will collide more often
- more collisions will be successful.

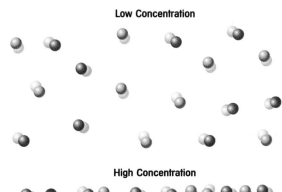

Low Concentration

(HT) Chemical reactions only occur when particles collide with each other with sufficient energy. This is called the **collision theory**. An increase in concentration and the number of particles results in more frequent collisions. So, there are more collisions which are sufficiently energetic for a reaction to occur.

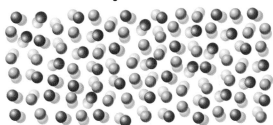

High Concentration

Key Words
Catalyst • Reactant

Chemical Synthesis

Surface Area of Solid Reactants

Large particles (for example, granulated solids) have a **small surface area** in relation to their volume which means that…

- fewer particles are exposed and available for collisions
- fewer successful collisions and a slower reaction.

Small particles (for example, powdered solids) have a **large surface area** in relation to their volume which means that…

- more particles are exposed and available for collisions
- more successful collisions and a faster reaction.

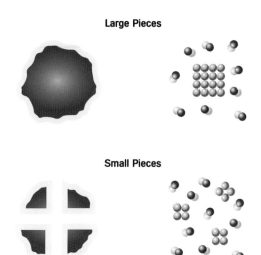

Large Pieces

Small Pieces

Using a Catalyst

Catalysts increase the rate of chemical reactions without being used up or changed during the process.

A catalyst…

- lowers the amount of energy needed for a successful collision
- makes more collisions successful
- speeds up the reaction.

Different reactions need different catalysts, e.g.…

- production of ammonia uses an iron catalyst
- production of sulfuric acid uses vanadium (V) oxide catalyst
- production of nitric acid uses platinum / rhodium gauze catalyst.

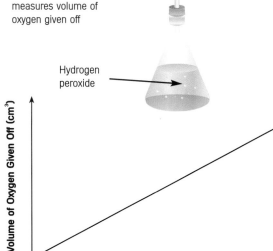

Without a Catalyst

Gas syringe measures volume of oxygen given off

Hydrogen peroxide

Volume of Oxygen Given Off (cm³)

Time (min)

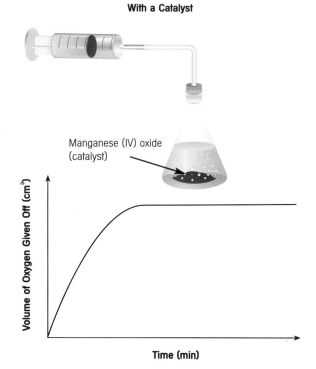

With a Catalyst

Manganese (IV) oxide (catalyst)

Volume of Oxygen Given Off (cm³)

Time (min)

Analysing the Rate of Reaction

Graphs can be plotted to show the progress of a chemical reaction. There are three things you need to remember:

- The steeper the line, the faster the reaction.
- When one of the **reactants** is used up the reaction stops (line becomes flat).
- The same amount of **product** is formed from the same amount of **reactants**, irrespective of rate.

The graph shows that reaction A is faster than reaction B. This could be because...

- the surface area of the solid reactants in reaction A is greater than in reaction B
- the temperature of reaction A is greater than reaction B
- the concentration of the solution in reaction A is greater than in reaction B
- a catalyst is used in reaction A but not in reaction B.

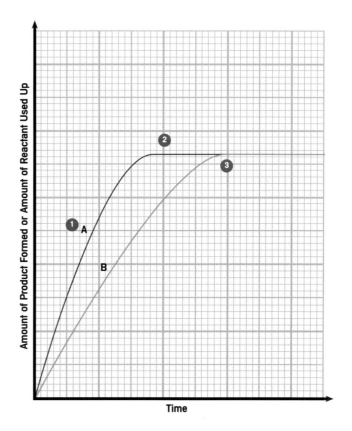

Controlling a Chemical Reaction

When carrying out a chemical synthesis on an industrial scale there are economic and safety factors to consider.

Examples of economic factors are as follows:
- The rate of manufacture must be high enough to produce a sufficient daily **yield** of product.
- Percentage yield must be high enough to produce a sufficient daily yield of product.
- A low percentage yield is acceptable providing the reaction can be repeated many times with recycled starting materials.
- Optimum conditions should be used that give the lowest cost rather than the fastest reaction or highest percentage yield.

Examples of safety factors are as follows:
- Care must be taken when using any of the reactants or products that could harm the environment if there was a leak.
- Care must be taken to avoid putting any harmful by-products into the environment.
- Complete risk assessment must be carried out, and the necessary precautions taken.

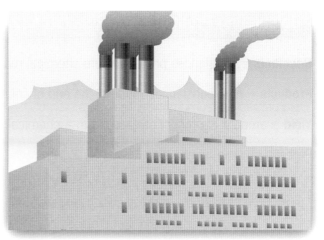

Key Words

Catalyst • Product • Reactant • Yield

Module C6 Summary

Acids and Alkalis

pH scale = measures acidity or alkalinity across a 14-point scale.

Acids ➡ pH less than 7

Alkali ➡ ph greater than 7

The pH of a substance can be measured using an indicator or pH meter.

Acidic compounds – produce aqueous **hydrogen** ions when dissolved in water.

Alkali compounds – produce aqueous **hydroxide** ions when dissolved in water.

Neutralisation

Acid + Base ⟶ Neutral salt solution + Water

Neutralisation ➡ remaining solution has neutral pH of 7.

Hydrogen ions from the acid react with hydroxide ions from the alkali to make water.

Making Salts

Acid + Metal hydroxide = Salt + Water

Acid + Metal oxide = Salt + Water

Acid + Metal carbonate = Salt + Water + Carbon dioxide

Acid + Metal = Salt + Hydrogen

Hydrochloric acid ➡ chloride salts.

Sulfuric acid ➡ sulphate salts.

Nitric acid ➡ nitrate salts.

Calculating Products and Reactants

Reactants = substances present before chemical reactions take place.

Products = new substances made at the end of chemicals reactions.

Yield = amount of product obtained from a chemical reaction.

Percentage yield compares…
- actual yield
- theoretical yield.

Relative atomic mass (A_r) = mass of one atom in comparison to mass of other atoms.

Relative formula mass (M_r) = relative atomic masses of all the elements added together.

Chemical Reactions

Chemical synthesis = process by which raw materials are made into useful products. Need to consider economic and safety factors when carrying it out on an industrial scale.

Titration – calculates the concentration of an acid by finding out how much alkali is needed to neutralise it.

Rates of Reactions

Rate of reaction = amount of reaction that takes place in given amount of time.

Rate of reaction can be found by…
* weighing reaction mixture
* measuring volume of gas produced
* observing formation of precipitate.

Rate of reaction is affected by…
* temperature
* concentration
* surface area
* catalysts.

Cold reaction mixture ➡ particles collide less often.

Hot reaction mixture ➡ particles collide more often.

Low concentration mixture ➡ particles collide less often.

High concentration mixture ➡ particles collide more often.

Large particles ➡ fewer successful collisions.

Small particles ➡ more successful collisions.

(HT) **Collision theory** = chemical reactions only occur when particles collide with each other with **sufficient energy**.

Catalysts = increase rate of reaction without being used up.

Analysing Rates of Reactions

Graphs can be plotted to show progress of chemical reactions.
* The steeper the graph, the faster the reaction.
* The line becomes flat when one of the reactants is used up.
* The same amount of product is formed from the same amount of reactants.

Module C6 Practice Questions

1 **a)** Complete the following general acid reactions.

    i) Acid + Alkali → Salt + ...

    ii) Acid + Metal carbonate → Salt + ... + Water

    iii) Acid + Metal oxide → Salt + ...

b) Draw lines between the boxes to match the acids to the salts they produce.

Sulfuric		Sulfates
Nitric		Chlorides
Hydrochloric		Nitrates

HT **2** Calcium carbonate and hydrochloric acid react together to produce calcium chloride, carbon dioxide and water.

a) Work out the relative formula mass, M_r, for each of the reactants and products shown in the equation and write them in the boxes. (A_r: Ca = 40, C = 12, O = 16, H = 1, Cl = 35.5.)

$$CaCO_3(s) \quad + \quad 2HCl(g) \quad \rightarrow \quad CaCl_2(aq) \quad + \quad CO_2(g) \quad + \quad H_2O(l)$$

i)	**ii)**	**iii)**	**iv)**	**v)**

b) What is the total mass of the substances on the left hand side? ....

c) What is the total mass of the substances on the right hand side? ....

d) Would you have expected the masses in parts **b)** and **c)** to be the same? Explain your answer.

....

....

e) What mass of calcium chloride can be produced from 2 grams of calcium carbonate?

....

f) Calculate the mass of water produced if a tonne of calcium carbonate is fully reacted with hydrochloric acid.

....

g) What mass of hydrochloric acid would be needed to fully react with 25 grams of calcium carbonate?

....

3 a) The concentration of an acid can be calculated by finding out how much alkali is needed to neutralise it. What is the name of this method?

b) Why is it important to use a pipette in this type of experiment?

c) What will happen to the indicator, phenolphthalein, when the acid is completely neutralised?

4 Circle the correct options in the following sentences:

a) In cold reactions particles move **quickly** / **slowly**. They **collide with** / **miss** each other less often. Less **movement** / **energy** means there are **more** / **fewer** successful collisions.

b) Large **molecules** / **particles** have a **large** / **small** surface area so there are fewer particles **covered up** / **exposed** and available for collision. **Increasing** / **reducing** surface area means there are more particles exposed and **available** / **unavailable** for collisions.

c) If the concentrations of **three** / **one** or both **reactants** / **products** are low, particles are **close together** / **spread out** and **miss** / **collide with** each other less often. If the concentration is increased the particles are **spread out** / **closer together** meaning there are **less** / **more** collisions.

5 If the rate of a chemical reaction is the speed at which a reaction occurs, list four ways in which you can change the rate of reaction.

a)   **b)**

c)   **d)**

6 The graph shows the results of three experiments where magnesium was reacted with hydrochloric acid. In each experiment a fair test was carried out.

a) Which line on the graph, **1**, **2** or **3**, shows the results of the experiment when the largest magnesium particles were used?

b) Explain you answer to part **a)**.

The Wave Model of Radiation

Types of Waves

Waves are regular patterns of disturbance that transfer energy from one point to another without transferring particles of matter.

There are two types of wave:
- **Longitudinal**.
- **Transverse**.

In **longitudinal waves**, each particle…
- vibrates to and fro about its normal position
- moves backwards and forwards in the same plane as the direction of wave movement.

Sound travels as longitudinal waves.

In **transverse waves**, each particle…
- vibrates up and down about its normal position
- moves up and down at right angles (90°) to the direction of wave movement.

Light and **water** ripples both travel as transverse waves.

In these diagrams, the movement of coils in a slinky spring is used to represent the movement of particles in waves.

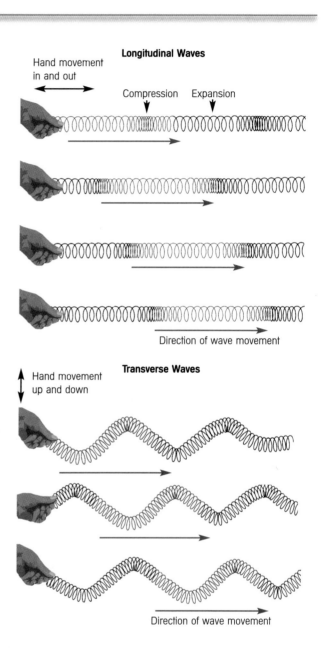

Wave Features

All waves have several important features:
- **Amplitude** – the maximum disturbance caused by a wave, measured by the distance from a crest (or trough) of the wave to the undisturbed position.
- **Wavelength** – the distance between corresponding points on two adjacent disturbances.
- **Frequency** – the number of waves produced, (or passing a particular point) in one second. Frequency is measured in **hertz** (Hz).

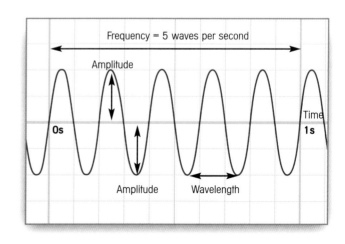

The Wave Model of Radiation

Wave Speed and Frequency

If a wave travels at a constant speed...
- **increasing** its frequency will **decrease** its wavelength
- **decreasing** its frequency will **increase** its wavelength.

If a wave has a constant frequency...
- **decreasing** its wave speed will **decrease** its wavelength
- **increasing** its wave speed will **increase** its wavelength.

N.B. The speed of a wave is usually independent of its frequency and amplitude.

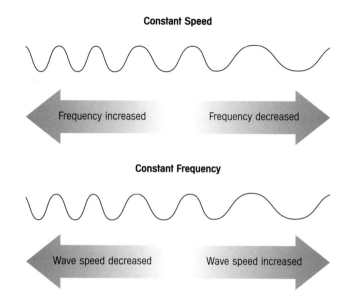

Constant Speed

Frequency increased   Frequency decreased

Constant Frequency

Wave speed decreased   Wave speed increased

The Wave Equation

Wave speed, frequency and wavelength are related by this formula:

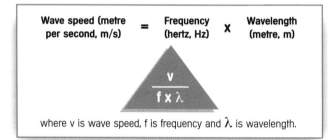

| Wave speed (metre per second, m/s) | = | Frequency (hertz, Hz) | x | Wavelength (metre, m) |

$$\frac{v}{f \times \lambda}$$

where v is wave speed, f is frequency and λ is wavelength.

Example

A tuning fork of frequency 480Hz produces sound waves with a wavelength of 70cm when it is tapped. What is the speed of the wave?

Wave speed = Frequency x Wavelength

= 480Hz x 0.7m

= **336m/s**

(HT) You can work out the frequency or wavelength by rearranging the wave speed formula.

Example

Radio 5 Live transmits on a frequency of 909 000Hz. If the speed of radio waves is 300 000 000m/s, on what wavelength does it transmit?

$$\text{Wavelength} = \frac{\text{Wave speed}}{\text{Frequency}}$$

$$= \frac{300\ 000\ 000\text{m/s}}{909\ 000\text{Hz}}$$

= **330m**

Key Words

Amplitude • Frequency • Longitudinal • Transverse • Wavelength

The Wave Model of Radiation

Behaviour of Waves

Light, water and sound waves can be…
- **reflected**
- **refracted**
- **diffracted**.

Reflection – Waves are reflected when a barrier is placed in their path. This effect can be seen in water waves.

Refraction – When waves cross a boundary between one medium and another, the **frequency** remains the same but there is a change in **wavelength**. This leads to a change in wave speed, which causes the wave to change direction.

Diffraction – When waves move through a narrow gap or past an obstacle they spread out from the edges. This is called diffraction. Diffraction is most obvious when…
- the size of the gap is similar to, or smaller than, the wavelength of the wave
- the waves which pass obstacles have long wavelengths.

Light waves need a very small gap to be diffracted.

The fact that light and sound can be diffracted provides evidence of their wave natures.

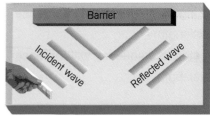

Reflection

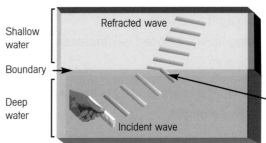

Refraction

Shallow water

Boundary

Deep water

Refracted wave

Incident wave

Change in direction due to change in wave speed

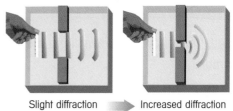

Diffraction

Slight diffraction → Increased diffraction

Diffraction

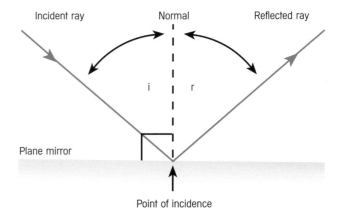

Slight diffraction → Increased diffraction

Reflection of Light

Light is **reflected** when it strikes a surface. This diagram shows light reflected in a plane mirror:
- The **normal line** is perpendicular to the reflecting surface at the point of incidence. It's used to calculate the angles of incidence and reflection.
- The **incident ray** is the light ray travelling **towards** the mirror.
- The **reflected ray** is the light ray travelling **away** from the mirror.

Angle of incidence	=	Angle of reflection

Incident ray   Normal   Reflected ray

i   r

Plane mirror

Point of incidence

→ = The direction the light ray travels in
i = angle of incidence
r = angle of reflection

Refraction of Light at an Interface

Light…
- changes direction when it crosses a boundary between one medium and another
- continues straight on when it meets the boundary at an angle of 90° (i.e. along the normal).

When the angle of refraction is **greater than 90°** the light can't escape from the medium and is reflected. This is called **total internal reflection**.

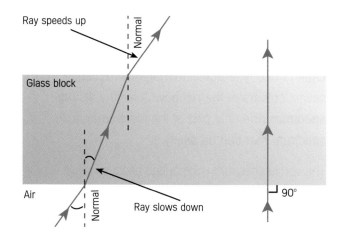

Ray speeds up

Normal

Glass block

Air

Normal

Ray slows down

90°

Interference

When two waves meet, their effects can add up. This is called interference.

Constructive interference is when…
- two waves arrive in step – the peak of one wave coincides with the peak of another
- the waves reinforce each other and their amplitudes add up.

Destructive interference is when…
- two waves arrive out of step – the peak of one wave meets the trough of another
- the waves cancel each other out.

Two rays of light can be shown to produce an **interference pattern**. If the light from one ray arriving at the screen is either **in step** or **out of step** with the other ray, it produces this pattern.

The interference of light and sound provides further evidence of their wave nature.

Waves in Step

Waves Out of Step

Interference Pattern

Key Words

Amplitude • Diffraction • Frequency • Interference • Reflection • Refraction • Wavelength

The Wave Model of Radiation

Electromagnetic Radiation

Electromagnetic radiations form the **electromagnetic spectrum**.

Light is one type of electromagnetic radiation. The seven 'colours of the rainbow' form the **visible spectrum** (the only part of the electromagnetic spectrum that can be seen).

The visible spectrum is produced because white light is made up of different colours. The colours are refracted by different amounts as they pass through a prism:
- Red light is refracted the least.
- Violet light is refracted the most.

This is because the different colours have…
- different frequencies
- different wavelengths.

The intensity of a beam of radiation depends on the number of photons (packets of energy) it delivers every second.

HT The intensity of the beam also depends on the **amount of energy** carried by each **photon**.

All electromagnetic waves travel through space (a vacuum) at the same, very high, speed.

Electromagnetic waves are very different from sound waves:
- Electromagnetic waves can travel through empty space.
- Sound waves need a medium (solid, liquid or gas) to travel through.

Key Words

Electromagnetic spectrum • Frequency • Photon • Reflection • Refraction • Wavelength

The Electromagnetic Spectrum

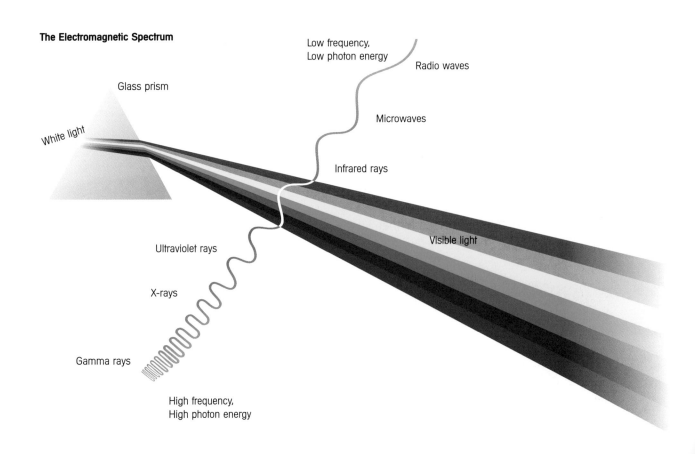

White light

Glass prism

Low frequency, Low photon energy

Radio waves

Microwaves

Infrared rays

Visible light

Ultraviolet rays

X-rays

Gamma rays

High frequency, High photon energy

Uses of Electromagnetic Waves

Different electromagnetic waves have **different frequencies**.

They can be used for different purposes depending on how much they are **reflected**, **absorbed** or **transmitted** by different materials.

Their signals can be carried by...
- radio waves and microwaves (through the Earth's atmosphere and space)
- light waves and infrared waves (through optical fibres).

Electromagnetic Waves	Properties and Uses
Radio waves 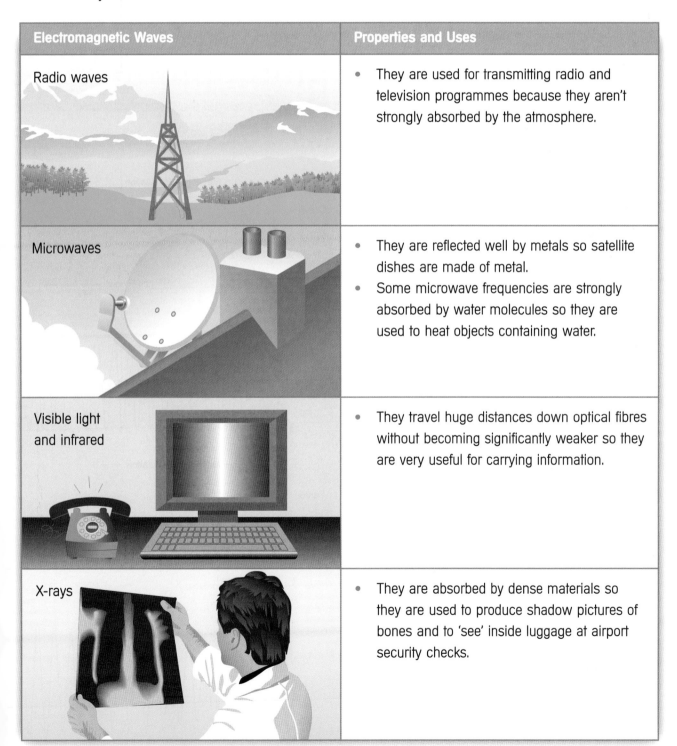	• They are used for transmitting radio and television programmes because they aren't strongly absorbed by the atmosphere.
Microwaves	• They are reflected well by metals so satellite dishes are made of metal. • Some microwave frequencies are strongly absorbed by water molecules so they are used to heat objects containing water.
Visible light and infrared	• They travel huge distances down optical fibres without becoming significantly weaker so they are very useful for carrying information.
X-rays	• They are absorbed by dense materials so they are used to produce shadow pictures of bones and to 'see' inside luggage at airport security checks.

The Wave Model of Radiation

Modulation

For a wave to carry a signal it must be **modulated**. This process involves making the wave vary either in **amplitude** or **frequency** to create a variation in the original wave. It's this pattern of variation that carries the information.

The pattern of variation is then decoded by the receiver to reproduce the original sound.

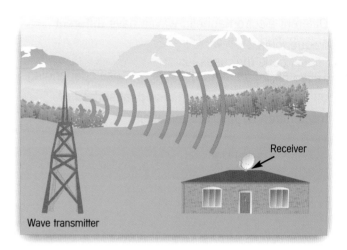

Receiver

Wave transmitter

Analogue Signals

In amplitude modulation or frequency modulation (AM or FM) the amplitude of the carrier wave is changed by the input signal.

With frequency modulation the input signal causes the frequency of the carrier wave to change.

In both these cases the signal is called an **analogue signal** because it varies in exactly the same way as the information it's carrying.

Frequency Modulation

Carrier

Signal

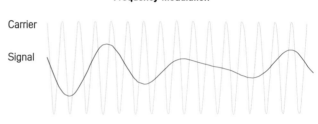

Output

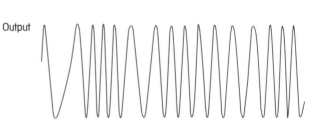

Amplitude Modulation

Carrier

Signal

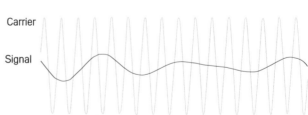

Output

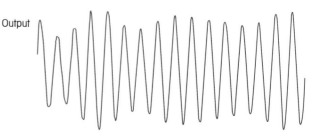

The Wave Model of Radiation

Digital Signals

Information, including sound, can also be transmitted digitally. The signal is converted into a digital code that uses just two symbols (0 and 1) which can then be transmitted as a series of short bursts of waves called **pulses** (0 = no pulse, i.e. off, 1 = pulse, i.e. on).

When the digital signal is received, the pulses are decoded to produce a copy of the original sound wave.

Benefits of Digital Signals

Both digital and analogue signals…
- become weaker (their amplitude becomes smaller) as they travel so they may have to be amplified at selected intervals
- can pick up random variations, called noise, which reduce the quality of the sound.

When a signal is amplified, any noise which has been picked up is also amplified.

Digital signals can travel long distances at a **higher quality** than analogue signals. This is because…
- **analogue signals** can have many different values so it's hard to distinguish between noise and the original signal. This means that noise can't be completely removed.
- **digital signals** only have two states, on (1) or off (0), so they can still be recognised despite any noise that's picked up. This means that any interference can be removed.

Analogue Signals

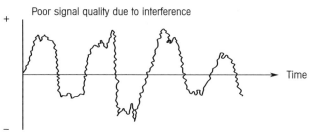

Poor signal quality due to interference

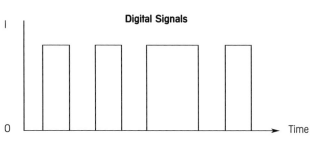

Digital Signals

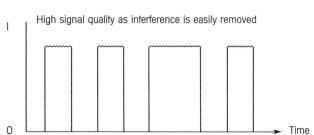

High signal quality as interference is easily removed

Key Words

Amplitude • Analogue • Digital • Frequency • Interference • Modulation

Module P6 Summary

Types of Waves

Waves = regular patterns of disturbance that transfer energy from one point to another without transferring particles of matter.

There are two types of waves:
- Longitudinal.
- Transverse.

Longitudinal waves ➡ particles vibrate to and fro.

Transverse waves ➡ particles vibrate up and down.

Wave Features

Amplitude = maximum disturbance caused by a wave.

Wavelength = distance between corresponding points on two adjacent disturbances.

Frequency = number of waves produced in one second. Measured in hertz.

If a wave travels at a constant speed…
- **increasing** frequency, **decreases** wavelength
- **decreasing** frequency, **increases** wavelength.

If a wave has a constant frequency…
- **increasing** wave speed, **increases** wavelength
- **decreasing** wave speed, **decreases** wavelength.

| Wave speed (metre per second, m/s) | = | Frequency (hertz, Hz) | X | Wavelength (metre, m) | $\dfrac{v}{f \times \lambda}$ |

where v is wave speed, f is frequency and λ is wavelength

Behaviour of Waves

Refraction = waves change direction when they pass between one medium and another.

Diffraction = waves spread out from the edges when they pass an obstacle or through a narrow gap.

Reflection = waves are reflected when a barrier is placed in their path.

Light

Light is reflected when it strikes a surface.

Incident ray = light travelling **towards** a surface.

Reflected ray = light travelling **away** from a surface.

Light…
- changes direction when it passes between one medium and another
- continues straight on when it meets a boundary at 90°.

Total internal reflection = light is reflected when the angle of refraction is greater than 90° as it can't escape from the medium.

Interference

Constructive interference = two waves arrive in step and reinforce each other.

Destructive interference = two waves arrive out of step and cancel each other out.

Interference pattern – caused when the light from one ray is either in step or out of step with the other ray.

Electromagnetic Radiation

Electromagnetic radiations form the **electromagnetic spectrum**.

Visible spectrum = the only part of the electromagnetic spectrum that can be seen.

Colours have…
- different frequencies
- different wavelengths.

Colours are refracted by different amounts as they pass through a prism:
- Red light ➡ refracted the least.
- Violet light ➡ refracted the most.

Photons = packets of energy.

HT Intensity of beam depends on **amount of energy** carried by each photon.

Electromagnetic waves can travel through empty space but sound waves need a medium to travel through.

Different electromagnetic waves have different **frequencies**.

Radio waves and microwaves ➡ travel through Earth's atmosphere and space.

Light waves and infrared waves ➡ travel through optical fibres.

Modulation

Modulation – makes a wave vary in amplitude or frequency to create a variation in the original wave.

The pattern of variation is decoded by a receiver to reproduce original sound.

Digital and Analogue Signals

Analogue signals = vary in exactly the same way as the information they carry. Can have many different values.

Digital signals = uses two symbols (0 = off and 1 = on) which can be transmitted as a series of pulses.

Digital signals can travel long distances at a higher quality than analogue signals because interference can be removed.

Module P6 Practice Questions

1 Fill in the missing words to complete the sentences below.

a) In .... waves, particles vibrate up and down about their normal position.

b) In .... waves, particles vibrate to and fro about their normal position.

2 Give the names of the parts labelled **A** and **B** on the diagram of a wave.

A ....   **B** ....

HT **3** A radio transmits signals with a wavelength of 200m at a speed of 300 000 000m/s. Calculate the frequency of the radio waves.

Wave speed (metre per second, m/s)	=	Frequency (hertz, Hz)	X	Wavelength (metre, m)

....

....

4 **a)** What happens when a wave is refracted?

....

....

....

b) Besides refraction, how else can obstacles alter the behaviour of sound, water and light waves? Tick the two correct options.

A Radiation ◯   **B** Reflection ◯

C Diffraction ◯   **D** Modulation ◯

5 **a)** What happens when the angle of light refraction is greater than 90°?

....

b) What is this called?

....

6 Explain how electromagnetic waves are different from sound waves.

....

....

7 Match the words **A, B, C** and **D** with their common uses numbered **1–4** below.

A Radio Waves   **B** Microwaves

C Light and Infrared Waves   **D** X-rays

1 Used to heat objects containing water. ⬭

2 Used for transmitting television programmes. ⬭

3 Used to 'see' inside luggage at airport security checks. ⬭

4 Used for carrying information. ⬭

8 **a)** Does the diagram below show an analogue signal or a digital signal? ....

b) Explain why digital signals are usually of better quality than analogue signals.

....

....

....

Glossary of Key Words

Acceleration – the rate at which an object increases in speed.

Acid – a compound that has a pH value lower than 7.

Alkali – a compound that has a pH value higher than 7.

Alkali metal – the six metals in Group 1 of the periodic table.

Alternating current (a.c.) – an electric current that changes direction of flow continuously.

Amplitude – the maximum disturbance caused by a wave.

Analogue – a signal that varies continuously in amplitude / frequency.

Atmosphere – the layer of gas surrounding the Earth.

Atom – the smallest part of an element which can enter into chemical reactions.

Axon – the thread-like extension of a nerve cell.

Biosphere – contains all living organisms on Earth.

Catalyst – a substance that increases the rate of a chemical reaction without being changed itself.

Central nervous system – the brain and spinal cord; allows organisms to react to their surroundings and coordinates their responses.

Cerebral cortex – the part of the human brain most concerned with intelligence, memory, language and consciousness.

Chromosome – a long molecule found in the nucleus of all cells containing DNA.

Clone – a genetically identical offspring of an organism.

Compound – a substance consisting of two or more substances chemically combined together.

Covalent bond – a bond between two atoms in which the atoms share one or more electrons.

Current – the rate of flow of an electrical charge, measured in amperes (A).

Denatured enzyme – an enzyme that has had its shape destroyed by heat and can no longer catalyse reactions.

Diatomic molecules – molecules that only exist in pairs of atoms.

Diffraction – the change in the direction of a wave at the edge of an obstacle in its path.

Diffusion – the movement of particles from an area of high concentration to an area of low concentration.

Digital – a signal which has an on / off state.

Direct current (d.c.) – an electric current that only flows in one direction.

Displacement – during a chemical reaction, a more reactive element will swap places with a less reactive element within a compound.

Distance–time graph – shows distance travelled against time taken; gradient represents speed.

DNA (Deoxyribonucleic Acid) – molecules that contain genetic information and make up chromosomes.

Effector – the part of the body, e.g. a muscle or a gland, which produces a response to a stimulus.

Efficiency – the ratio of energy output to energy input, expressed as a percentage.

Electrolysis – the process by which an electric current causes a solution to undergo chemical decomposition.

Electrolyte – the molten or aqueous solution of an ionic compound used in electrolysis.

Electromagnetic spectrum – a continuous arrangement that displays electromagnetic waves in order of increasing frequency.

Electron – a negatively charged particle found orbiting the nucleus of an atom.

Element – a substance that consists of only one type of atom.

Embryo – a ball of cells which will develop into a human / animal baby.

Enzyme – a protein which speeds up the rate of reaction in living organisms (a catalyst in living things).

Fertilisation – the fusion of the male gamete with the female gamete.

Force – a push or pull acting upon an object.

Frequency – the number of waves produced (or that pass a particular point) in one second.

Friction – the resistive force between two surfaces as they move past each other.

Gamete – a specialised sex cell formed by meiosis.

Gene – a small section of DNA of a chromosome which determines a particular characteristic.

Gradient – the steepness of the slope of a graph.

Gravity – a force of attraction between all masses.

Group – a vertical column of elements in the periodic table.

Halogen – one of the five non-metals in Group 7 of the periodic table.

Homeostasis – the maintenance of a constant internal environment.

Hydrosphere – contains all the water on Earth including rivers, oceans, lakes etc.

Hypothermia – an uncontrolled decrease in body temperature.

Incubator – a container that controls temperature and oxygen levels to help premature babies to survive.

Instantaneous speed – the speed of an object at a particular point.

Interference – the noise created when two waves meet, either in step or out of step.

Ion – a particle that has a positive or negative electrical charge.

Ionic bond – the process by which two or more atoms lose or gain electrons to become charged ions.

Kinetic energy – the energy possessed by an object due to its movement.

Lithosphere – the rigid outer layer of the Earth made up of the crust and the part of the mantle just below it.

Longitudinal – an energy-carrying wave in which the movement of the particles is in line with the direction in which the energy is being transferred.

Meiosis – the cell division that forms daughter cells with half the number of chromosomes as the parent cell.

Meristem – an area where unspecialised cells divide, producing plant growth.

Mitosis – the cell division that forms two daughter cells, each with the same number of chromosomes as the parent cell.

Modulation – making a wave vary either in amplitude or frequency to create a variation in the original wave.

Momentum – a measure of state of motion of an object as a product of its mass and velocity.

Neuron – a specialised cell which transmits electrical messages or nerve impulses when stimulated.

Neutralisation – a reaction between an acid and a base which forms a neutral solution.

Neutron – a particle found in the nucleus of atoms that has no electric charge.

Nucleus (biology) – the control centre of a cell.

Nucleus (chemistry) – the small central core of an atom, consisting of protons and neutrons.

Ore – a naturally occurring mineral, from which it is economically viable to extract a metal.

Organelles – the different parts of a cell's structure.

Osmosis – the movement of water from a dilute to a more concentrated solution across a partially permeable membrane.

Glossary of Key Words

Period – a horizontal row of elements in the periodic table.

Photon – a packet of energy.

Phototropism – a plant's response to light.

Potential difference / voltage – the difference in electrical charge between two charged points.

Product – the substance made at the end of a chemical reaction.

Proton – a positively charged particle found in the nucleus of atoms.

Reactant – one of the substances present before a chemical reaction takes place.

Receptor – the part of the nervous system that detects a stimulus.

Reflection – a wave that is thrown back from a surface.

Reflex action – a fast, automatic response.

Refraction – the change in direction of a wave as it passes from one medium to another.

Relative atomic mass (A_r) – the average mass of an atom of an element compared to $\frac{1}{12}$ of a carbon atom.

Relative Formula Mass (M_r) – the sum of the atomic masses of all atoms in a molecule.

Resistance – the opposition to the flow of an electric current.

Resultant force – the total force acting on an object (the effect of all the forces combined).

Ribosome – a small structure found in the cytoplasm of living cells, where protein synthesis takes place.

Static electricity – the electricity produced by friction.

Stem cell – a cell of a human embryo or adult bone marrow which has the ability to differentiate.

Stimulus – a change in an organism's environment.

Synapse – a small gap between adjacent neurons.

Titration – a method used to find the concentration of an acid or alkali.

Transformer – an electrical device used to change the voltage of alternating current.

Transverse – a wave in which the vibrations are at $90°$ to the direction of energy transfer.

Urea – the toxins produced when proteins are broken down.

Velocity – an object's speed and direction.

Velocity–time graph – shows velocity against time taken; gradient represents acceleration.

Voltage / potential difference – the difference in electrical charge between two charged points.

Wavelength – the distance between corresponding points on two adjacent disturbances.

Yield – the amount of product obtained from a reaction.

Zygote – a cell formed by the fusion of the nuclei of a male sex cell and female sex cell (gametes).

(HT) **Active site** – the place where the molecule fits into the enzyme.

Active transport – the movement of a substance against a concentration gradient.

Anti-diuretic hormone (ADH) – a hormone that controls the concentration of urine.

Auxin – a plant hormone that affects the growth and development of a plant.

Hypothalamus – the part of the brain responsible for maintaining homeostasis.

Pituitary gland – the small gland at the base of the brain that produces hormones.

Vasoconstriction – the narrowing of the blood vessels to decrease heat loss from the surface of the skin.

Vasodilation – the widening of the blood vessels to increase heat loss from the surface of the skin.

Module B4

1. maintenance; constant; environment.
2. Death will rapidly follow.
3. B and C
4. A
5. **a) i)–ii) in any order:** Blood oxygen levels; Salt levels.
   b) i)–ii) in any order: Scuba diving; Mountain climbing.
6. **a)** A 4; B 1; C 2; D 3
   b) The maintenance of a steady state by reversing the change in conditions.
7. **a)–c) in any order:** Oxygen; Carbon dioxide; Dissolved food.

8. **a) and b)**

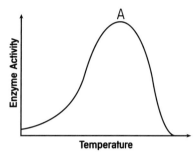

   c) It is where an enzyme is permanently destroyed and stops working.
9. Vasodilation – Hot conditions; Vasoconstriction – Cold conditions
10. C
11. **a)** Kidneys
    b) iii)
12. A small amount of concentrated urine will be produced.

Module C4

1. The group number corresponds to the number of electrons in the outer energy level and the period number corresponds to how many energy levels there are.
2. **a)** Proton
   b) +1
   c) 1
   d) Electron
   e) -1
3. A Nucleus; B Electron; C Shell.
4. Corrosive = lithium, fluorine, sodium hydroxide; Flammable = lithium, fluorine; Irritant = chlorine; Toxic = none.
5. **a)** To bleach dyes and kill bacteria in water.
   i)– ii) any two from; Wear safety glasses; Work in a fume cupboard; Work in a well ventilated room; Use small amounts of very dilute concentrations; Avoid working near naked flame; Watch demonstrations very carefully.
6. In the halogens the outer shell gets further away from the nucleus so an electron is less easily gained.

7. **a)**   Sodium Atom   Chlorine Atom

   b) i) It loses its outer electron   **ii)** It gains an extra electron
   c)   Sodium Chloride

    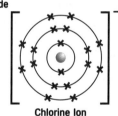

        Sodium Ion   Chlorine Ion
8. **a)** Ag^+ **b)** NO_3^- **c)** Al^{3+} **d)** Cl^- **e)** $AlCl_3$ **f)** Al^{3+} **g)** SO_4^{2-} **h)** $Al_2(SO_4)_3$

Module P4

1. **a)–b) in any order:** Speed; Direction of travel.
2. $\frac{20m}{5s}$ = 4m/s
3. The speed of an object at a particular point in time.
4. **a)** A 3; B 2; C 1.
   b) $\frac{20m}{4s}$ = 5m/s
5. To make sure drivers don't exceed the speed limit and that they rest for suitable amounts of time.
6. The resistive force between two objects as they slide past one another.
7. add up; subtract; resultant force.

8. 1500kg x 45m/s = 67 500kg m/s
9. **a) i)–iii) any three from:** Seat belts; Crumple zones; Motorcycle and bicycle helmets; Air bags.
   b) They increase the time of impact.
10. C
11. $\frac{1}{2}$ x 1200kg x $(12m/s)^2$ = $\frac{1}{2}$ x 1200 x 144 = 86 400J
12. It remains the same.
13. **a)** 18N x 8m = 144J
    b) 144J
    c) 144 = $\frac{1}{2}$ x 2kg x V^2
        144 = V^2
        V = $\sqrt{144}$
          = 12m/s

Answers to Practice Questions

Module B5

1. **a)** A Cell membrane; B Cytoplasm; C Ribosome; D Nucleus.
    b) Protein synthesis occurs.
2. A 4; C 3; D 2.
3. **a)–b) in any order:** Testes; Ovaries.
4. Zygote
5. **a) i)** T **ii)** G **iii)** C **iv)** A
    b) mRNA is a smaller copy that is small enough to leave.
6. **a)** Three
    b) Twenty
7. **a)** They are unspecialised and can turn into any kind of cell.

    b) The cells will have become specialised.
8. Meristems
9. **a)** Responsible for transporting dissolved food up and down the plant.
    b) Responsible for transporting water and dissolved minerals from the roots to the leaves.
10. **a)** **Drawing needs to show a shoot curving to face the light**.
    b) i) **The letter A should be in middle of the shoot tip**.
       ii) On the curved surface furthest away from the light, i.e. left hand side.
11. It makes them grow faster.

Module C5

1. **a)** atmosphere; gas.
    b) water; compounds.
    c) biosphere; organisms; animals.
    d) lithosphere; outer; Earth; crust; mantle.
2. **a)** Lithosphere
    b) Nitrogen is returned to the lithosphere.
    c) By denitrifying bacteria.
3. **a)** The electrons in the covalent bond are closer to the oxygen atom than the hydrogen atom, resulting in a polar molecule.
    b) The forces between the molecules are slightly stronger than with other covalent molecules due to the small charges on the atoms.
    c) The small charges on the atoms in the water molecule attract the charges on the ions.
4. A, B and C.

5. **a)–c) in any order:** Carbohydrates; Proteins; DNA.
6. **a)** External forces cause layers of metal ions to move by sliding over other layers.
    b) Electrons are free to move throughout the structure. When an electrical force is applied, the electrons move along the metal in one direction.
    c) A lot of energy is needed to break the strong force of attraction between the metal ions and the sea of electrons.
7. A 5; B 2; C 4; D 6; E 1; F 7; G 3.

Module P5

1. **a)** The two materials will repel each other.
    b) The two materials will attract each other.
2. ⊣├─
3. **a)** Direct; Alternating.
    b) i)–ii) in any order: It's easier to generate; It can be distributed more efficiently.
4. **a)** Voltage
    b) Greater
5. **a)** $\frac{15V}{5A} = 3\Omega$
    b) 0.6A x 20Ω = 12V
    c) More energy is transferred from the charge flowing through a greater resistance because it takes more energy to push the current through the resistor.
6. **a)–b) in any order:** Moving the magnet out of the coil; Moving the other pole of the magnet into the coil.

7. **a)** To change the voltage of an alternating current.
    b) When two coils of wire are close to each other, a changing magnetic field in one coil can induce a voltage in the other. Alternating current flowing through the primary coil creates an alternating magnetic field which induces an alternating current in the secondary coil.
    c) 20V
8. **a)** Joules
    b) Because a joule is a very small amount of energy.
    c) 40W x 30s = 1200J
    d) 1.8kW x 0.5h = 0.9kWh
9. **a)** $\frac{1600}{2000}$ x 100 = 80%
    b) $\frac{60}{200}$ x 100 = 30%
    c) $\frac{260}{400}$ x 100 = 65%

Answers to Practice Questions

Module B6

1. **a)** Central nervous system
   b) Peripheral nervous system
   c) Central nervous system
2. **a)** Sensory neuron
   b) Motor neuron
3. It causes the gland to release a hormone into the blood.
4. **a)–b) in any order:** It insulates the neuron; It increases the speed at which the impulse travels.
5. Synapses are the gaps between adjacent neurons.
6. A 4; B 2; C 3.

7. Stepping reflex – Baby makes walking movements with legs when held under arms in an upright position.
   Startle (Moro) reflex – Baby shoots out arms and legs when startled.
   Grasping Reflex – Baby tightly grasps a finger that is placed in its hand.
   Rooting Reflex – Baby turns head and opens mouth when its cheek is stroked.
   Sucking Reflex – Baby sucks on a finger that is put into its mouth.
8. C
9. **a)–b) in any order:** Electroencephalogram (EEG); Magnetic Resonance Imaging (MRI)
10. Feral children
11. They change the speed at which nerve impulses travel to the brain.
12. Ecstasy (MDMA)

Module C6

1. **a)** **i)** Water
      ii) Carbon dioxide
      iii) Water
   b) Sulfuric – sulfates; Nitric – nitrates; Hydrochloric – chlorides.
2. **a)** **i)** $40 + 12 + 3 \times 16 = 100$
      ii) $2 \times (1 + 35.5) = 73$
      iii) $40 + (2 \times 35.5) = 111$
      iv) $12 + (2 \times 16) = 44$
      v) $(2 \times 1) + 16 = 18$
   b) 173
   c) 173
   d) Yes. Conservation of mass means that no mass is lost or gained during a reaction and there is exactly the same number of atoms in the total products as there was in the total reactants.
   e) 100 gram of $CaCO_3$ = 111 gram of $CaCl_2$
      2 gram of $CaCO_3$ = $(\frac{2}{100})$ × 111 gram of $CaCl_2$ = 2.22 gram of $CaCl_2$
      (Alternative: amount of $CaCO_3$ = $\frac{100}{2}$ = 50 times smaller
      Amount of $CaCl_2$ = $\frac{111}{50}$ = 2.22 grams)

   f) 1 tonne = 1000 kg
      100 gram of $CaCO_3$ = 18 gram of H_2O
      mass of water produced = 180 kg
   g) 100 gram of $CaCO_3$ + 73 gram of HCl
      $\frac{25}{100} = \frac{1}{4}$ so need $\frac{1}{4}$ of 73 for HCl = 18.25g
3. **a)** Titration.
   b) So that you will always know the amount of acid used.
   c) The indicator will be completely pink.
4. **a)** slowly; collide with; energy; fewer.
   b) particles; small; exposed; increasing; available.
   c) one; reactants; spread out; collide with; closer together; more.
5. **a)–d) in any order:** Changing the temperature; Changing the concentration; Changing the surface area; Using a catalyst.
6. **a)** 3
   b) Large particles have a small surface area. A small surface area means a slower reaction.

Module P6

1. **a)** Transverse
   b) Longitudinal.
2. A Amplitude; B Wavelength.
3. Frequency = $\frac{300\,000\,000\,m/s}{200m}$ = 1 500 000Hz
4. **a)** A wave is refracted when it crosses a boundary between one medium and another. The wave's frequency stays the same, but there is a change in wavelength. This leads to a change in wave speed, which causes the wave to change direction.
   b) B and C

5. **a)** The light can't escape from the medium and is reflected.
   b) Total internal reflection.
6. Electromagnetic waves can travel through empty space but sound waves need a medium (solid, liquid or gas) to travel through.
7. 1 B; 2 A; 3 D; 4 C.
8. **a)** Digital signal
   b) Because digital signals only have two states, on (1) or off (0), so they can still be recognised despite any noise that's picked up. This means any interference can be removed.

Index